CAT IQ

TRAINING

UNLEASH YOUR PURRFECT FRIEND'S POTENTIAL THROUGH SMART TECHNIQUES

MELANIE ALVARADO

TABLE OF CONTENTS

YOUR FREE GIFT

As a way of saying thanks for your purchase, I'm offering the book: "From Whiskers to Fame: Ten Cats Who Made History" for FREE to my readers.

To get instant access just go to:

bit.ly/tencatswhomadehistory

Inside the book you will discover the ways in which cats have left their indelible mark on civilizations and continue to do so today.

Yours truly,
Melanie

Introduction

"I had been told that the training procedure with cats was difficult. It's not. Mine had me trained in two days."

– Bill Dana

When I brought Kiki home from the animal shelter, I knew I was in for a challenge. The adorable domestic short hair turned out to be one sassy feline. Within a week, her tiny claws had ripped the fabric of my couch exposing the inner padding while the scratching post lay abandoned nearby.

Her 3 a.m. zoomies and desire to topple everything in sight left me at my wit's end. Soon, she replaced the need for me to set an alarm for the mornings. Hours before I was supposed to get up, she'd pounce on the bed, startling me awake! Needless to say, I had to think of some way of reigning in her wild urges, or remain anxious and sleep-deprived. Little did I know of the struggle that lay ahead. The innocent kitten that I'd fallen in love with at the animal shelter quickly proved to be one tough cookie.

Of course, I'd forget it all when she'd curl up in my arms and purr lovingly. So giving up on her was never an option. Still, her stubborn refusal to be trained had me scratching my head. If only I could get the tiny furball to stop causing such mayhem!

When all else failed, I became determined to take matters into my own hands and study feline behavior in more detail. As I pored over books, I gained valuable insight into the psychology of my feline companion. Eventually, my research helped me devise positive reinforcement techniques that have benefitted numerous pet owners.

Ten years after adopting Kiki, I look back at those chaotic early days and feel a sense of pride at how much she's mellowed out. Gone are the days when she used to tear my couch to shreds or knock over random objects. She's learned to curb her destructive urges, expressing her instincts in positive ways while remaining as playful and energetic as ever.

It's been years since I brought Kiki home and a lot has changed. For one, she's no longer the only cat in the house. Four more feline friends have joined her since then. The only difference is that I now enjoy their harmless antics without worrying about the state of the house.

My name is Melanie Alvarado, and I'm a devoted cat lover and certified feline behaviorist with over a decade of experience. My goal is to help pet owners understand their cat's behavior and train them. In my decade-long experience working with cat owners, I've seen it all. So, I know there's no such thing as a pet that simply can't be trained.

Oftentimes the problem lies in not understanding what your cat is trying to communicate to you. And like most problems that seem incredibly complex at first sight, there are solutions that guarantee positive results. This is why the best part about my job is seeing my clients develop a healthy, loving relationship with their pets without fretting about unwanted behaviors.

Cat IQ Training will help you unlock the mysterious world of cats. You'll learn what's going on in your cat's mind and what you can do to fulfill your cat's needs. By the time you finish reading this book, you'll find yourself ready to take any challenge related to your pet head on and transform them into a well-behaved, intelligent, and satisfied companion.

The techniques outlined in this book will help you to:

- **Get Rid of Unwanted Behaviors:** No more shredded furniture, overturned objects, and predawn disturbances.
- **Strengthen Your Connection:** Deepen the bond between you and your cat, so there's less stress, more cuddles, and playtime!
- **Increase Your Cat's Well-being:** Happy cats are well-behaved cats. You'll learn how to answer your pets' requirements, so it doesn't feel the need to act out.

As a cat enthusiast, it gives me immense joy to help owners understand these remarkable creatures. I have observed firsthand the impact of understanding cat behaviors and effective training in improving the relationship between cats and their owners.

Cat IQ Training will help you decipher your cats' unique personality, understand their many quirks, and effectively train them. With this book, my goal is to share tried and true methods with you, so you can tame your feisty feline and experience the joy of having a cheerful, well-trained cat by your side.

As I write this, Kiki sits sprawled out on the window sill. Her luminous eyes watch the people passing by on the sidewalk. My other cat, Zoe, is busy playing with her toy mouse while Charlie and Coco have settled in for an evening nap on the couch beside me. Nothing compares to the unconditional love that these majestic creatures possess for their owners. It has the power to heal us in our darkest times and make even the bleakest circumstances a little better. As the famous French poet, Anatole France, rightly said, "Until one has loved an animal, a part of one's soul remains unawakened."

It's time to discover the astonishing potential of your feline friend. Let's delve into the captivating world of cat behavior and training. Time to cast your doubts aside and set off on a cat-tastic adventure!

1

Understanding Cat Behavior

"A cat has absolute emotional honesty: human beings,
for one reason or another, may hide their feelings,
but a cat does not."

– Ernest Hemingway

Your cat is trying to tell you something. The positioning of its tail, its fixed stare, and tense posture are some small gestures it uses to communicate. It's up to you to decode your magnificent feline's subtle clues. If you've ever looked into your cat's glowing eyes and wondered what's going on inside its mind, then you've come to the right place.

You no longer have to feel puzzled by your cat's behavior. Contrary to popular belief, cats are pretty straightforward creatures. Whatever they're feeling, they make it a point to let you know. The problem is that we rarely pay attention to their cues. So let's take a closer look at cat instincts and unravel the secrets of the feline mind.

Feline Instincts Explained

Remember, they weren't always this cute and harmless. Their ancestors prowled through the savannah, hunting down wild animals. They reigned supreme in the jungles and leaped across mountainous terrain, their mighty roars resounding for miles. While years of domestication may have watered down your cat's predatory past, remnants of those times remain engraved in its mind.

You see glimpses of your cat's ferocious ancestors every now and then. The way it crouches low, wiggles its rear, and becomes extremely still before pouncing on a toy. Reduced to raging battles on their soft toys, occasional displays of aggression are small reminders of the glory days.

Hunting Aficionados

Kiki had a habit of bringing me the most unusual gifts. She'd place a dead mouse or a bird at my feet and look up expectantly as if waiting for me to shower her with praise. Needless to say, the tiny trophies she'd lovingly present me with would make my stomach turn. Why did she keep doing that? Why was she intent on making me lose my appetite?

Hunting is an important cat instinct. With the food bowl filled to the brim, domestic cats no longer feel the need to go out in search of food for their young. While your cat may no longer rely on its hunting skills for survival, the occasional trophies it presents you with could be a sign of affection. Cats bring their prey home if they feel safe, comfortable, and secure. Another reason is that they want to share their prize with their family! Could there be a greater compliment?

Practicing its hunting skills remains important for its well-being. However, if dead animals are simply not your cup of tea no matter how sweet the gesture may be, there are ways to redirect your cat's behavior. Here are some ways you can fulfill your ferocious furball's desire to experience the excitement of being on the hunt.

- **Stalking and Chasing:** Hide treats in your house or outside in the garden so your cat can sniff them out and practice its hunting instincts.
- **Chase and Capture:** Use moving toys to play with your cat. Watch them crouch low, focus on their prey,

and pounce! It's best to use toys that are large and soft, making them an easy target.

How can you prevent your cat from bringing you such grisly presents? The first misconception that owners tend to have about this issue is that their cat is simply hungry. However, this isn't always the case. From an evolutionary standpoint, cats have an innate desire to hunt whenever possible, whether they feel hungry or not. That being said, if the sight of dead animals makes you queasy, then there's a lot you can do to curb your cat's killer instincts.

1. Satisfy their hunting desire through play. Providing mental stimulation in this manner will help redirect your cat's hunting instinct. Feather teasers or moving toys are excellent options and may even prevent other destructive urges such as biting or pouncing on your feet.
2. Make sure they're getting a balanced diet. Some cats may resort to going outside for a hunt because they're not receiving adequate nutrition. Try giving them smaller, more frequent meals throughout, and make sure to fulfill their nutritional requirements.
3. Keep them indoors during high activity times. Hunting expeditions mostly take place around dawn or dusk when small mammals or birds are out searching for a snack.

Territorial Titans

Once Kiki started feeling nice and comfortable in her new home, I noticed a strange habit. She kept rubbing or scratching different corners and furniture. It wasn't until I started learning about cat behaviors that I understood what she was doing. Cats are territorial beings that mark their space with their scent, either by scratching, rubbing, or a little tinkle! In short, Kiki was marking her kingdom to ward off other cats that might try to take her place.

Grooming Buffs

Cats love to spruce themselves up! Grooming achieves more than just making them look good. It maintains healthy fur by encouraging the production of sebum, an oily secretion formed by the sebaceous glands at the base of their hair. As your cat licks its fur, it spreads the sebum over its hair coat, lubricating and protecting it. This also removes dirt, loose hair, parasites like fleas, and prevents matting.

It's important to note that grooming is also an indication of good feline health. A disheveled appearance could be a result of illness. It may not be possible for old, arthritic, or obese cats to fold themselves into pretzels to lick themselves clean. On the other hand, emotional stress such as pain or anxiety can lead to excessive grooming behavior such as constantly picking at a bald spot. If your sick or elderly cat stops grooming regularly, gently brush its coat. If the hair is extremely matted, then it's best to have it looked at by a professional.

Taking Cues from Your Cat

Kiki is perched atop the table, eyes lit up, pupils dilated. What is she about to do? If you've familiarized yourself with cat instincts, then you can tell that Kiki is in hunting mode. A moment later, she leaps in the air, her tiny claws close around the toy bird on the floor. She wriggles on the mat, pretending to fight her formidable enemy and preventing it from making an escape.

Gaining insight into your cat's mind helps you understand and respond to their natural instincts. The better you're able to read your cat's behavior, the better you get at predicting its actions by understanding its motivations. This will prove invaluable in the long run as you get around to training them.

Paying attention to your cat's gestures also helps you pick up on important clues, so you can nip problems in the bud. Take note of the ears, head, tense muscles, and the eyes for signs of discomfort. Crouching, excessive grooming, and grumpiness could be signs of stress. Likewise, keep a lookout for unusual behaviors. For instance, if your cat is used to leaping off the furniture, but now puts its paw on the surface first before jumping, it could point to underlying health issues such as arthritis.

Here are some reasons why understanding cat behavior is the cornerstone of cat training.

Behavior Prediction

Once you have a good grasp of your pet's instincts, you can anticipate its actions. Awareness of animal psychology helps us design effective strategies to redirect their energy and find positive outlets for their wild urges.

For example, your cat may roll on its back, exposing its tummy. This is a sign of vulnerability and shows that your feline companion trusts you. Generally, relaxed posture, constricted pupils, and forward-facing ears indicate calm. Meanwhile, tense muscles, crouching low to the ground, and dilated pupils show that your cat feels threatened.

Preventing Behavioral Problems

Knowledge of feline instincts places you in a better position to prevent or address common behavioral problems. For example, if your cat continues to prefer your furniture over its scratching post, try sprinkling catnip at the base or hanging it in a small bag on top. It may just encourage your cat to give up gnawing at the couch.

Creating a Positive Environment

Using play, puzzles, and interactive toys to satisfy your cat's impulses enriches their environment. A mentally stimulating home leads to emotional satisfaction. Happy cats are not only healthier but also live longer. They make loyal and calm companions, exhibiting fewer problems. Keeping your cat in a carefree state of feline bliss could just be the solution you've been looking for.

Positive Reinforcement Strategies

You're sitting on the couch with your cat in your lap. You're petting it gently when its tail starts to twitch. You ignore it and continue to scratch its soft fur. The twitching increases. Pretty soon they're intently staring at your hand. Just when you least expect it, they lash out. The tiny claws scratch your skin and they go after your hand for a little nibble. Ouch! What's gotten into your four-legged friend? What upset them so much when you were just being nice? Is it time to bring out the squirt bottle to discipline your pet?

Generally, cats prefer brief but frequent interactions. They like being petted around the head and the face where their scent glands are instead of areas near the tail or the tummy. Your cat launched into attack mode to make you stop. It's the only way for it to communicate how it feels.

While there's an abundance of research on dog training methods, cats haven't been studied to the same extent. From what extensive research on dogs shows us, severe punishments or harsh training methods like squirting water cause emotional upset, giving rise to fear, anxiety, and aggression. It also deteriorates their relationship with their owners. There's no reason for us to believe it would be any different for cats.

Let's take a moment to analyze the repercussions of using the squirt bottle. A jet of cool water in the cat's face can make them quite stressed. Ironically, they may associate the feeling of discomfort not with their action but with the person subjecting them to this punishment. Numerous studies suggest that owners who punish their pets are more likely to witness more difficulties.

So, if you're looking for long term solutions, do yourself a favor and chuck the squirt bottles and shake cans in the trash. Avoid clapping, yelling, or other means to startle or frighten your pet. Remember, a stressed or anxious cat will always prove more difficult to train. Not to mention, there's little evidence that such methods will help you achieve the required results.

On the other hand, positive reinforcement techniques guarantee improvement in cat behavior without compromising their relationship with their owners. The best course of action is to train your feline friend gradually. Spend a few minutes each day, and slowly increase the time as you go along. Present them with treats whenever they behave positively to encourage good behavior.

In the next few chapters, we'll look more closely at these techniques and how they can be used to solve a vast number of cat-related problems.

The Takeaway

You can't read your cat's mind, but you can take a good guess based on their cues. Detecting and responding to the first signs of distress can help resolve major behavioral problems. Understanding your feline friend's instincts is the first step to establishing a meaningful relationship with your pet. The more accurately you comprehend your cat's attempts at communication, the more success you'll have in preventing destructive outcomes by providing positive alternatives. With the right techniques, you can make purr-fect behavior a reality!

2

Preparing for Cat Training

"In the eyes of a cat, all things belong to cats."
— English proverb

Convincing myself to head over to the rescue center and adopt Kiki took some time. My mind was buzzing with questions about how I'd care for her. Where would she sleep? What would she eat? What things would she need? I just didn't know where to start!

If you find yourself in a similar headspace, don't worry because I've got you covered. In this chapter, we're going to start with the very first step: cat-proofing your home. Cats are curious creatures, so it's no wonder you find them getting into all kinds of trouble around the house.

You can't expect your pet to be mindful of keeping your place in order, if they're tempted at every turn. Having an untrained cat in your home means your curtains, prized heirlooms, and expensive decor are all fair game. And while your fearless feline may seem invincible, it can seriously hurt itself in the process. This is why cat-proofing your house is crucial.

Of all the cat breeds, Bengals, Savannahs, and Maine Coons are the most capable of stirring up serious mischief. Partly because they're so sharp! They can even learn to open doors! Naturally, kittens of any breed are tiny furballs bursting with energy, making them a bit of a handful.

The key to keeping your stress levels to a bare minimum while caring for your untamed tabbies and frisky kittens is to provide them with a safe environment. It's the only way to ensure your cat's safety while minimizing damage to your home during the early stages of training.

Cat-Proofing Your Home One Room At A Time

Shortly after bringing her home, the electric cord in my living room became Kiki's favorite. Once I had that sorted, she became obsessed with the curtain tiebacks. As soon as I'd get rid of a potential hazard, she'd move on to a new target. So I decided to go all in and remove every conceivable threat. It didn't take me long to realize that I couldn't do so from my vantage point. I had to see things from Kiki's perspective, which meant getting on all fours to examine my surroundings.

It might seem strange, but it's necessary to do so. After all, the same practice is recommended for parents looking to baby-proof their homes, and cats are more or less the same as tiny crawling explorers. This way you won't miss possible dangers that could have escaped your notice otherwise.

Here are some things you should keep in mind as you set out to turn your house into a safe haven for your cat:

- Take your cat's perspective into account. Get down to their level and observe your surroundings to root out potential hazards.
- Limit access to dangerous areas. Make sure windows and balconies are screened to prevent accidental falls.
- Be mindful of electrical safety.
- Keep fragile and precious items in sturdy display cabinets or areas that your pet can't access.
- Remove toxic substances, making sure they're stored safely and out of your cat's reach.

- Create cozy hideaways for your kitty. These places will increase their sense of security. Something as simple as an upturned wicker basket or a woolen cave bed could become your cat's favorite place.
- Keep an eye on your whiskered friend, especially during the early stages of training. They need plenty of positive reinforcement to redirect their actions.

Now that we've discussed the basics of creating a cat-friendly environment, let's look at different areas in our house and what we can do to make them more secure:

Living Room

- **Blind and curtain cords have got to go.** Either tie them up or cut them. Your ever curious feline can get tangled in the cords, which could lead to strangulation. If possible, go for curtains or blinds with looped cords to prevent the problem altogether.
- **Use flameless candles or place them up high.** You don't want your curious feline roaming around flames they can knock over. Burned or singed whiskers and tails can be avoided by replacing wax candles with flameless ones, so you can keep your pet safe without compromising on the ambiance.
- **Secure electrical cords.** Nibbling on electrical cords, phone chargers, and cables are common cat hobbies. Wrap them up with cord protectors or tape them to the floor with double-sided tape, the stickiness will discourage your cat from toying with them.

- **Put away essential oils and potpourri.** Certain essential oils in liquid potpourri can be toxic for pets, so it's better to steer clear from simmer pots, diffusers, or potpourri burners.
- **Remove poisonous plants or flowers.** Don't be surprised if you catch your cat nibbling on your plants every now and then; it's a common habit that can cause serious medical issues. Cyclamens, sago palms, lilies, and dumb cane are some plants that can cause serious problems if ingested.
- **Secure unsteady or heavy furniture to the wall.** Wobbly shelves, flat screen TVs, or anything that poses a risk of toppling over due to your cat's antics needs to be anchored.
- **Protect your furniture.** Cover your sofa or keep the scratching post nearby to divert your kitten. If possible, get rid of recliners because small pets often get trapped underneath, leading to injuries.

Bedroom/Home Office

- **Declutter your nightstand.** Put away your jars of skincare, hair ties, or medication if you don't want your ever inquisitive cat pawing through your stuff.
- **Keep mothballs out of reach.** Smelling or ingesting these can be toxic for cats. Lock the drawers or cabinets that you store them in or toss them in the trash.
- **Power off the paper shredder.** Unplug or switch the shredder off when you're done. You don't want your cat's tail or paws anywhere near those sharp blades.

Kitchen

- **Secure cupboards and pantry doors.** This will prevent your cat from creeping into the cleaning closet, pawing through bottles of chemicals, or spilling food from the pantry. Child-proof locks on cabinet doors are the best option for keeping your groceries and cleaning supplies out of reach of your sneaky cats.
- **Keep the trash, compost, or recycling bin covered.** You can count on your untrained cat to rummage through your trash. However, they can suffocate in food bags or become sick from eating decaying foods. So keep the lid tightly shut or place the bins somewhere your cat won't be able to access.
- **Cover the stovetop.** Use burner covers to prevent your cat from landing on the hot stove.
- **Put away sharp objects.** Magnetic knife racks might make you feel like a professional chef, but they're not the safest option for cats. Also, make sure to store scissors and razors in drawers to avoid any accidents.

Bathroom

- **Secure wastebaskets.** Like any other string, cats love playing with used dental floss, which could lead to digestive problems.
- **Keep the lid down on the toilet.** If you have a jumpy kitten roaming around the house, then you'd better make sure to keep the toilet lid closed at all times. Avoid leaving toilet cleaners in the bowl, automatic bowl cleaners, or cakes.

Laundry Room/Shed/Garage

- **Keep the dryer closed and always check before using.** The toasty dryer compartment may seem like a comfy place for your cat to take a snooze, but it could prove fatal if you don't double check before deciding to do the laundry.
- **Store motor oils, antifreeze, and windshield fluids in a safe place.** A few licks of these chemicals could be lethal.
- **Keep rock salts or ice melters out of reach of your furry friends.** Choose pet-safe options because most salt-based ice melts can lead to stomach problems or burn your cat's paws.

Your Training Toolkit

Once I had the house prepped and ready, it was time to move on to my training toolkit. Getting a hold of Kiki's attention was tricky. After a few frustrating weeks, I became convinced I needed a magic wand to solve my problems.

Slowly, reality started to sink in: there was no quick fix or magical solution. After weeks of failing to reign in Kiki, I realized what I was lacking. I couldn't get my hands on a magic wand, but I could buy the next best thing—or set of things—to help me transform my sassy feline. Salvation came in the form of a list of tools that helped me grab Kiki's attention but also redirect and reward positive behaviors. Finally, I was off to a good start!

On that note, let's look at all the tools and equipment that will come in handy for taming your cat. Here are all the items you'll need to make your cat feel at home:

Food Pouches

The cornerstone of cat training is offering rewards. Treats should be high-value, small in size, and have a low-calorie count. Choose snacks that your cat loves or your feisty feline may not consider the reward worth the effort. They should be about the size of a pea, offering a quick bite. You don't want your kitten to become preoccupied with chomping down a huge meal during training sessions.

The treats should be low in calories. Typically, the total amount of treats shouldn't exceed more than 10% of your pet's daily caloric intake. Otherwise, your cat could end up gaining a significant amount of weight. For example, twenty to twenty five high-caloric treats each day could lead to considerable weight gain. I used freeze-dried raw treats crumbled into smaller sizes that are big on protein but low in calories for training my cats.

Once you've decided on the treat, drop by your nearest pet store to grab a food pouch. These nifty little devices are great for storing small snacks for your kitty and can be clipped to your clothes, ensuring easy access. They're particularly useful during training sessions and if your cat is persistent about getting rewards for good behavior throughout the day.

Look for pouches that are easy to clean, portable, and accessible. You'll need something that conceals the treats and keeps them secure so your cat doesn't launch an attack. Pouches with magnetic closures are a great solution for cat's that are treat thieves. Choose a pouch made with material that is easy to clean. Frequent rinsing is necessary even if you're using dry treats because they tend to leave oil residue, which can mix with dust particles. I used a silicone food pouch for Kiki that had a magnetic closure and that I could clip to my waistband.

Clicker Device

Say hello to your new best friend! It's the closest thing you'll find to a magic wand. A clicker device is a valuable tool for correcting your cat's behavior. The distinct clicking sound will help capture your cat's attention the moment it acts the way that's required. You can follow this with a treat so your cat associates the action with a reward.

Make sure to choose one that is small and relatively quiet, so you don't startle your cat. They usually come with a wrist strap so you can keep it with you at all times. Still, I think it'll be helpful to have a bunch of them in your house. You can keep them stashed in every room or carry them in your pocket, so you always have them on hand. Keep a few of them as backup in case the one you have gets damaged or lost.

Toys and Puzzle Feeders

Your American shorthair or Russian blue may not know the thrill of racing through the wild, but you still need to keep its feline mind occupied by recreating a similar scenario. Interactive toys and puzzle feeders provide the mental stimulation that every cat desires. Not only do they keep your cat busy, they also offer rewards, promoting problem-solving skills.

Such toys are excellent for stimulating your cat's natural foraging instincts. Batting its paws at the pegs of a feeder puzzle to find hidden treats satisfies your furry friend's desire to hunt. Most puzzles come with different difficulty settings, so you can keep your cat interested for a long time.

Scratching Posts and Cat Trees

Your cat needs a place where it can lounge and let loose its natural instincts. Scratching posts and cat trees allow your cat to climb and scratch to its heart's content. Make sure that the structure is sturdy, stable, and made with good material that isn't prone to excessive shedding.

Look for items that have a good height, feature vertical and horizontal surfaces, and contain a variety of textures. Typically, cats prefer strong material they can shred with their claws. A loud scratching noise could make the experience more satisfying for them. Search for material that is different from the textures you already have in your home like carpets. Your cat may feel more drawn to its scratching post, if it offers an element of novelty. Moreover, carpets don't always provide the most satisfying experience as they tend to be rather rough.

Sisal fabric is a heavy duty material that makes a great scratching surface. You can find it in the form of rope or fabric. Your cat can easily run its claws down the fabric while getting a good grip on the material. While sisal rope doesn't offer an uninterrupted vertical shredding motion, the bumpy texture and mild resistance make it more appealing to cats.

Another material you'll frequently find is cardboard, a cat favorite. It's sturdy and creates a lot of scratching noise. You can find it attached on angled or flat surfaces in addition to hollow tubes. Lastly, if you want a scratching post that your cat could also lounge on, look for varieties featuring perches or condos.

As for cat trees, you should take your cat's age and your home space into consideration before going out to buy one. Senior cats may prefer a structure that allows ample space for them to lounge. Kittens, on the other hand, are filled with curiosity and buzzing with energy. A more elaborate set up with multiple levels may appeal to them more.

The size of the cat tree that you choose ultimately depends on the space available around your house. Cat trees can be simple or complex, ranging from small to large. They're especially useful if you have kittens to stimulate their development.

Investing in cat trees that come with scratching posts will allow your cat to experience the best of both worlds! These two-in-one structures are cost effective and take up less room, making them the perfect choice for people on a budget with limited space.

Litter Box

They might all look the same but not all litter boxes suit all cats. Don't be surprised if you find your kitty showing strong preferences for the shape, size, and depth of its litter box. Some cats might feel spooked by automatic scooping options while others detest hoods and lids. We'll discuss these feline likes and dislikes in more detail in Chapter 4.

When it comes to size, bigger is usually better. The length of the litter box should be 1 ½ times the length of your cat, measuring from the nose to the tail. This way the litter box will be big enough for your cat to easily get inside, move around, scratch, and do its business. You can use concrete mixing trays or storage containers as alternatives; however, keep in mind that older cats will require a low entry point.

Harness and Leash

Kiki is an adventurer! I can't keep her housebound for too long. That being said, our first few trips outside proved to be a lot more exhausting than I'd expected. She'd whizz out of sight every chance she got, and I'd have to spend hours searching for her. Getting a harness helped me limit her escapades while allowing her to explore her surroundings.

Cat harnesses are not the same as dog harnesses which are made for broader shoulders and may be too big for your cat. Feline harnesses are more delicate with more cushioning material, offering a more streamlined fit and providing greater comfort. Keep in mind that cats move differently as compared to dogs. A harness specifically designed for cats gives them the freedom to move, making it less likely that they'd resist wearing a leash.

There are various types of cat harnesses available; however, h-harnesses and figure-of-eights remain the most popular. You may have to experiment with different types before you find the best one for your kitty. Similarly, there are numerous kinds of leashes to choose from, ranging from more rigid to rather flexible ones. Deciding what to choose depends on how much control you require on your cat. A flexible leash works well for more adventurous cats while a firmer one is usually the best choice for cats that require more control.

Grooming Supplies

Cats are regal beings that enjoy being looked after. Grooming can be an excellent bonding activity between you and your feline. Brushes and combs help keep their luscious fur coat in top notch condition. Some things you'll need include

- **Slicker Brush:** Great for getting rid of mats and tangles, especially for long-haired cats.
- **Bristle Brush:** Works best for short-haired cats to distribute natural oils and remove loose fur.
- **Fine Toothed Comb:** Excellent for detangling and cleaning debris.
- **Nail Clippers/ Trimmers:** Necessary for keeping those sharp claws in check!
- **Shampoo:** Go for ones specifically designed for cats to avoid skin flare ups.
- **Flea Comb:** To rid your cat's fur of those pesky fleas and flea eggs.
- **Ear Cleaners:** These include special solutions to clean their ears and avoid infection. However, make sure to consult your vet before deciding what to buy.
- **Toothbrush/Toothpaste:** Necessary for maintaining oral hygiene.
- **Wipes:** For quick spot cleaning or removing discharge around the eyes.

- **Grooming Gloves/Mitts:** So you can remove loose fur while petting your whiskered friend.

Setting Realistic Targets

Kiki wasn't going to change overnight. The sooner I realized this, the more I was able to focus my attention on daily small wins. Sometimes it's important to take a step back and look at the whole picture. Whatever little progress you make toward your goal counts. Small, achievable targets will allow you to set up a realistic road map. Having reasonable expectations from your cat means you won't get disheartened and stay committed to achieving your goals.

There's no question that your cat is intelligent and capable of learning; however, they will proceed at their own pace. Overwhelming your cat with hours of training may prove counterproductive in many ways. Here are a few tips to approach training with the correct mindset:

- **No two cats are the same:** Just like humans, each cat has a unique personality. What worked for your neighbor's Siamese might not work for your Maine Coon. Practice patience and modify your training methods depending on your cat's response.
- **Small steps for the win:** Training is a gradual process, requiring patience and persistence. Instead of seeking instant perfection, opt for incremental progress. Celebrate the small victories as stepping stones, bringing you closer to your goals.

- **Repeat, reinforce, and reward:** Repetition is a core aspect of pet training. Cats and dogs learn through repetitive attempts consistently carried out over a period of time. So, be prepared to repeat, reinforce, and reward desired behaviors until they become ingrained habits.
- **Positive attitude:** Focus on creating a positive relationship with your cat through training. Teaching your cat new tricks should be an enjoyable experience for both of you. Keep the training sessions light and fun. A happy cat is more cooperative and open to learning than a grumpy one.

The Takeaway

Cat proofing your home is a fail-safe method to remove any hurdles you may encounter while training your spirited feline. Take time to analyze each room, paying special attention to any place or object that may pose a risk to a curious kitten or a dauntless tomcat. Try to adopt a different perspective as you explore your surroundings for potential hazards.

The right training tools and supplies can make all the difference when it comes to cat training. Getting your hands on proper training equipment can help prevent mishaps and ensure your cat's security. Setting realistic expectations will help you lay the groundwork for successful training without feeling discouraged by minor setbacks.

Once you've made all the arrangements listed above, you're all set to kick off your cat training journey one paw at a time!

3

Basic Obedience Training

"In ancient times cats were worshiped as gods; they
have not forgotten this."
– Terry Pratchett

One look at Kiki and you're convinced you're in the presence of royalty. Look a little longer and you can almost imagine a crown atop her head! How do you get a cat with such a regal aura to obey? It may seem like a useless exercise.

Indeed, it seemed that way in the beginning. My enthusiastic attempts to train her were met with cold indifference. I'd ask her to sit and she'd give me a glare. I'd hold my hand up for a high-five and she'd simply swish her tail. At times, I could imagine her rolling her eyes and groaning, "Are you serious?"

Kiki's icy reception to my training waned my enthusiasm a little; however, I was determined not to give up. I just had to figure out some way to get past the cattitude and get my cat interested.

"Many cats love training if done properly, with patience and rewards," says Katenna Jones, behaviorist and director of Jones Animal Behavior in Rhode Island (Hodgson, 2022). The quote caught me by surprise. I'd turned to the internet for answers and was surprised to learn that experts believed cats were just as fun to train as dogs.

It made me do a double take at Kiki sulking on the couch after a failed training session. That can't be right, I thought to myself as I read about the joys of cat training. Finally, it hit me. The problem lay in my approach.

Surprisingly, cats take well to training if the lessons are fun and offer plenty of rewards. Moreover, having a strong bond with your pet increases your chances of success.

Although cats can't be trained to perform numerous tricks like dogs, basic training requires little effort. However, they're naturally better at learning to use the litter box and avoiding aggressive behaviors while playing.

Most of the time, all it takes to prevent certain behaviors in cats is simply to not provoke them. For example, if your cat keeps pulling on the leash, try a harness rather than a training collar. A harness is less likely to trigger a frantic response, which could lead to choking. If your cat's prone to taking a nibble at you, try redirecting its predatory instincts to a toy.

The advantages of cat training outweigh the effort required in the beginning. "Training provides mental and physical stimulation as well as positive social contact," says Jones. "Just the act of training in and of itself is incredibly valuable for frustrated, bored, shy, and fearful cats."

Behaviorist Stanley Coren likens dogs to toddlers and cats to teenagers. While a few words of kindness or a mere gesture of affection is enough to encourage a dog to cooperate, cats need more incentives to stay motivated. The prospect of rewards could snap your cat out of a grouchy mood and make them willing to participate.

Let's look at the basics of obedience training and how you can turn your stubborn cat into a happy camper.

How to Train Your Feline

Cats may not be the first creatures to jump to mind when you come across the words: *animal training*. However, they're extremely intelligent animals, and teaching them can be an enjoyable experience for both of you.

As I learned with Kiki, tweaking my methods had an enormous effect. Soon, Kiki started responding to my cues. A few months of regular training sessions and she'd learned a number of tricks, something that had seemed impossible when I was starting out. Here are a few tricks that your kitty will be able to pick up on in no time.

Sit

Teaching your imperious cat to sit on command is a huge achievement and a great starting point. The simple trick can prove useful in various circumstances, from making mealtimes hassle free to preventing your tiny adventurer from darting outside.

Choose a quiet area free from distractions. Hold a treat close to your cat's nose, gradually raising it above its head. As their eyes follow the treat, they naturally assume a sitting position. The instant they do so, say "sit" and reward them with a treat. Shower them with lots of praise and continue practicing regularly.

In addition to the above, you can also use the clicker each time your cat sits naturally and present them with a reward. Pretty soon they'll be sitting on cue as soon as you show them a treat. Start using the word "sit" when it seems likely they're about to do so to strengthen their association of the word with a treat. Click and offer a treat as soon as they assume this pose as frequently as possible. The clicking and reward cycle should taper off naturally as your cat begins responding instinctively to your cues.

Stay

This is a valuable skill to teach cats patience and self-control. Initially, I struggled to get my feline Flash to stay put. A few weeks of consistent practice helped calm her down and resist bolting out the door at the slightest provocation.

Begin by instructing your cat to sit. Hold up your hand with the palm toward your cat's face and say "stay." Step back and observe what your cat does. If it keeps sitting, offer a reward. Encourage your cat to stay a bit longer by taking more steps away from them while holding your hand up. Keep increasing the distance and duration that your cat should stay put before offering them a treat.

You can also use a mat, towel, or napkin to teach this trick. Whenever your cat steps on the mat, use the clicker and say "On your mat" or "Stay." If the cat stays put for a few seconds, offer a treat. Gradually, increase the duration as before. Once your cat has mastered this trick, you can use the mat to get them to stay in the cat tree or any other location.

Come

Keeping Kiki restricted to the house was close to impossible. She'd shoot out of the house every chance she got, climbing trees and chasing squirrels until she lost her way. Teaching her to respond to my call helped ease the stress. I no longer had to go searching for her around the neighborhood and could trust her to show up after she'd had her fill of adventure.

As before, choose a quiet area in your home with minimal distractions. Kneel and call your cat's name along with the command "come." Make sure to use a cheery tone, so your cat approaches you expecting a reward. Practice regularly, trying it out in different locations and with an increasing level of distractions.

Your cats may rush toward you the second you step in through the door. Use these moments as an opportunity to train them. Say the word "come" and present them with a treat. You can also use the clicker and reward your cat whenever it dashes toward you. The goal is to decrease the use of the clicker and rewards over time as the association between the command word and the action becomes second nature.

Gentle Play

You're petting your beloved cat, gently stroking their coat when–Ouch–they take a nip at your fingers! What is up with that? Does your cat hate you?

Before you take offense, keep in mind that there are many reasons behind the little nibble at your fingers or toes. If you're dealing with kittens, it could be due to teething. If your cat is depressed or scared, they could be conveying their anger or frustration. It could also be a love bite! Yes, it could be the only way for your cat to show affection when they're overstimulated.

Regardless of why your cat tries to take a munch at you, there are ways to prevent such behavior. Dab a bit of store-bought or homemade treat paste on your knuckles. Allow your kitten to lick it off your hand while repeating the word "Gentle." Calmly pull your hand away if they begin to bite.

Other ways to discourage roughhousing during play include praising and rewarding gentle behavior. Quietly disengage if your cat gets toothy. Offer rewards whenever they use their paws instead of claws during playtime. Whenever your cat does use its teeth, give it a stuffed toy for it to chew on instead.

Keep in mind that play fighting is a crucial part of cat development. It allows them to practice their natural hunting instincts. Even though it is normal cat behavior, we shouldn't give them the impression that it's okay to bite or scratch their owners.

Redirecting them toward more appropriate outlets is one of numerous ways to counter this. Moreover, it is also important to respect your cat's space and read their body language. Discerning your cat's feelings through their gestures allows you to pinpoint the causes of aggression and prevent them from lashing out.

Target

Another way to encourage your cat to follow instructions and respond to your call is to teach them to target. You can easily find a target wand at your local pet store or make one yourself. It is quite simply a lightweight stick with a ball at the tip. Commercially available ones are usually foldable and extendable, fitting easily in your pocket.

These helpful tools are used to teach your pet to move on your command. It provides a clear visual target that cats can follow. You can even find types that function as both clicker and target stick. The ball end of some of these wands allows you to put snacks inside to make training easier. However, you can also use lickable treats if you like.

Hold the wand two inches from your cat. As soon as it touches it, say the word "Target" and offer a reward. Use it to move your cat from one place to another. As your cat learns to respond to these cues, you can use the target stick to encourage it to get inside the cat carrier by using the prompt "In the box," which brings us to our next trick.

In the Box

While most cats jump into the carrier happily, others may put up a fight. In addition to using the target stick, there are several other ways to teach your cat to be less fussy. Place treats inside the carrier and say the words "In the box" when your cat goes inside.

Positive Reinforcement Techniques

In the end, the road to Kiki's heart was through a bag of flavored cat treats. All she wanted was heaps of praise, served with a couple of freeze-dried shrimp treats on the side. As it turns out, cats respond best to the language of love. And what better way is there to show love than by giving them their favorite food?

Positive reinforcement is the foundation of cat training. It is the most effective and humane technique that guarantees results. Here are some tips to include this method in your training routine:

Choose Irresistible Rewards

Your connoisseur cat should feel excited about the treats you choose. However, nutritional benefits are just as important as taste preferences. Avoid snacks packed with unnecessary carbohydrates and preservatives that lack a decent amount of protein. Ironically, a lot of dental cat treats end up causing more harm than good. Anything that is loaded with carbohydrates and leaves a starchy residue is bad news for your cat's canines. Moreover, such snacks only add on the pounds while doing nothing to satisfy their hunger.

Some cats might prefer being cuddled or a toy instead of a quick bite. Tailor your reward keeping your pet's preferences in mind, so they remain interested in the training process. Pay attention to what motivates your feline and choose rewards wisely.

Getting the Timing Right

Timing is everything! Reward your cat as soon as they perform the desired behavior. Using the clicker is like taking a snapshot of appropriate behavior. For successful training, it's important to click at the precise moment your cat displays the correct action. When a particular action is repeatedly rewarded, it becomes a habit.

Another great tip is to schedule your sessions before mealtimes. Cats are more willing to learn when they're a little hungry. This way they'll feel more excited about the rewards.

Keep Sessions Short

Your clever cat has a short attention span. Limit sessions to 5 - 10 minutes to minimize building up boredom or frustration. Schedule several of such short sessions throughout the day. Be patient and consistent. Use the same commands and signals to avoid confusion. Make sure all family members follow the same rules and involve them in training. Patience and persistence are your greatest strengths during this process.

Offer Multiple Treats

There is no universal treat that will work its magic on your cat. Cats, like humans, have different preferences. A dry treat or kibble may be all it takes to get some cats looking forward to their training sessions. Others may appreciate wet foods or squeezable treats. Likewise, you may find that your sassy Siamese is more willing to follow your lead when you offer chin scratches or playtime.

In addition to choosing treats based on your pet's preferences, you can combine multiple rewards to keep things interesting. You can also offer different treats for different difficulty levels. Reserve higher-value treats for more complicated tasks; however, remember that this doesn't necessarily mean a more expensive snack, but simply anything that gets your cat excited.

Common Training Challenges

Training Kiki tested me like never before. Mostly because I jumped into it without knowing what to expect. The hurdles I encountered along the way frequently threw me off balance. It would take some time for me to pick up where I left off with the same fervor as before.

By the time I was on cat number three, I'd mastered the game. Looking back, I can see how I could've easily avoided most of the problems I experienced. Here are some common challenges you'll most likely run into while taming your spirited cat and strategies to overcome them:

Lack of Interest

Kiki stares out the window while I dance around with the target stick. She lets out a huge yawn before giving me a bored look. Her disinterest often had me wondering whether I was teaching her to sit or Advanced Algebra! If you can't seem to hold your cat's attention for more than a few seconds, there are ways to fix it.

Perhaps your cat isn't interested in the rewards you have to offer or it's simply distracted by what's going on outside the window. Try a different reward, make sure they're hungry if you're working with snacks, or teach at a different time when they're not tired or sleepy. Experiment with different rewards and train in a quiet area.

Repeatedly presenting the same toys may be contributing to your feline's declining interest. To avoid this, you can hide the toys somewhere for a few days and reintroduce them or rotate the toys available in their space so they don't get used to them.

As with toddlers, cats are distracted easily. While choosing an area free from distractions works initially, you should gradually desensitize your cat to distractions so they're prepared to respond to your call in every environment.

Other reasons for your cat's waning interest could be that they're not feeling well or the task is too complicated for them. Sessions that last longer than fifteen minutes can make cats feel overwhelmed and build up frustration. If things continue going south, try taking a break for a day or two before resuming regular training.

Tackling Aggressive Behavior

Watch out for signs of aggression. Despite your best efforts, sometimes it's impossible to read your pet's mind. If you miss the signs, your docile kitty might surprise you by lashing out. Reasons for their sudden outbursts could include frustration or feeling overwhelmed. Recognizing early signs of aggression or distress are crucial to prevent bites or scratches.

Keep an eye on your cat's head, face, and body posture. Dilated pupils, flattened ears, drooping whiskers, tail tucked under the body, and chin turned up are some signs of trouble brewing under the surface. Bringing out the clicker at these moments may not be the most productive.

Plateauing Progress

What to do when progress stalls? Your cat loses interest and doesn't respond to new command words? Is there only a set number of tricks that each cat can learn? When you hit a plateau in training, it's important not to lose confidence and keep going. Sometimes a short break is all it takes to get your feline fighter back in the ring. If problems persist, use the time to go over the basics. Reinforce previous tricks before introducing new challenges.

Striking A Fine Balance

Work and play go hand-in-hand. Cats love being challenged, but they also need downtime to recharge and get back in the game. Balance training sessions with playtime to avoid burnout. Another aspect that most cat owners tend to ignore while training is allowing energy outlets for their pets. The aim of training your cat is not to suppress their animal instincts but to find healthy and positive outlets for them.

Cats need areas where they can scratch, jump, and climb to their heart's delight. Providing them with such outlets keeps them feeling happy, minimizes destructive behaviors, and keeps them entertained. Scratching posts, puzzle feeders, toys, and outdoor play present opportunities for cats to act on their basic instincts. Such stress relieving exercises instill a level of calm, making your feisty feline more willing to follow your lead.

The Takeaway

The first steps are usually the hardest. Start with small, fairly simple tasks and slowly build your way up to more challenging ones. Basic obedience techniques such as sit, stay, and come can be used in a variety of different ways to ensure cat safety.

Positive reinforcement plays a crucial role in pet training. Your cat needs plenty of love to nudge it onward in its training journey. Put thought into the treats you offer, keeping your pet's preferences in mind, and present them with a variety of different rewards.

Keep in mind that it won't always be smooth sailing. Take challenges head on and be prepared to bounce back. Maintain a positive mindset, stay patient, and consistent and you'll have a well-behaved and responsive cat in no time!

4

Litter Box Training

"Cats are connoisseurs of comfort."
– James Herriot

Kiki was a tough pupil, resisting most of what I tried to teach her. So you can imagine my surprise when she was trotting off to the litter box within a few days. Cats have a natural inclination to use the litter box, making the training process a whole lot easier than with dogs. While it may take some time for puppies to get the hang of using the litter box, most kittens will be heading off to theirs within a few days.

Essential Supplies For Litter Box Training

Before you begin, make sure to gather your supplies. You'll need a litter box, cat litter, and a scoop. As I mentioned in Chapter 2, litter boxes come in a variety of styles. These include covered spaces to corner-shaped boxes aimed at maximizing space and privacy.

Moreover, they vary according to your cat's breed, weight, and age. As I stated before, a general rule of thumb is that the container should be one half the length of your cat so it can get inside and relieve itself comfortably.

Similarly, there are various options of litter available in the market. Clumping litter tends to be the most popular due to its ability to prevent the particles from binding together when wet. Another convenient tool to invest in is a sifting scoop, so you can lift the mess and get rid of it rather than changing the whole litter.

Here are some things you need to consider before your cat gets its paws in the litter tray:

Getting the Right Litter

Cats are picky creatures. You can count on them to refuse to use anything that's not up to their standards. Some may prefer non-clumping varieties while others might enjoy the clumping kind. Choosing the right litter for your cat is a trial and error process. You'll have to experiment with different varieties until you find the one that pleases your furry friend.

While the choice comes down to your cat's preference, it's helpful to know the options available in the market. Non-clumping litters soak up large volumes of liquid and cancel out unpleasant odors. This means the tray remains fresh and usable for a week or more as long as solid wastes are removed.

Clumping litter, on the other hand, allows clumps to form around solid and liquid waste, requiring more thorough and frequent cleaning. Since all the particles in the litter tend to get contaminated, you'll have to change and empty the entire tray to refresh it.

Coarse-grained, non-clumping litter is the go-to option for kittens. Being the inquisitive creatures they are, they tend to nibble on everything. The coarse particles cause less problems if ingested. However, you can switch to other options once your cat is a year old. Keep in mind that the transition requires time.

Finding the Right Container

Choosing the right container is just as important as getting the litter right. Most cats dislike covered boxes because they can block their vision, preventing them from looking out for potential dangers. Older cats may struggle to climb in and out of a box with high walls. Additionally, you need to position the litter box in a quiet area with minimal distractions, so your cat won't be disturbed.

Most litter boxes include a rectangular plastic bin. Modifications to this model include top entry varieties to contain the litter, low or automatic entrances specifically designed for senior cats. Generally, cats love looking at their surroundings while they use the bathroom; however, a box that is too open could create a mess on the floor. Litter boxes with high sides can prevent this problem, but don't expect them to work for elderly cats that experience trouble climbing.

If litter particles spilling over is a concern, you can opt for open top containers that come with a shield. Lastly, if your cat prefers a bit of privacy while doing its business, you can go for top entry litter boxes. The entrance into these boxes is from the top through the lid. Cats jump out of the opening when they're done, so litter doesn't scatter on the floor. Top entry boxes prevent cats from observing their surroundings, making it somewhat of an acquired taste.

How Many Are Too Many

If you have three or more cats, a single litter box will not do. Each cat should have its own litter box plus one extra. If you're on a budget, you can upcycle any container big enough for your cat to move around and dig. Just make sure there are no sharp edges that could cause possible injuries if you carve out an entrance. Moreover, the container should be sturdy and prevent spillage.

Bear in mind that cats have high standards, so you'll have to scoop often. Your cat won't appreciate it if you ignore your cleaning duties. If your feline master starts going to the bathroom too frequently, it's best to have a spare box ready with clean litter inside.

How to Litter Train Your Cat

Once you've assembled all the necessary items, it's time to step into the arena and confront your whiskered opponent. The first step is to help your furry friend get accustomed to the litter box by simply placing it near them and allowing them to explore. Let them get inside, dig around, and get used to it.

Schedule training exercises after naps and mealtimes when your cat will most likely feel the need to relieve itself. Use the target stick to get your cat into the litter box. Place the box in a quiet corner around the house away from the areas where your cat eats. Most cats don't like to go to the bathroom in the same spot where they have their mealtimes.

Layer two inches of litter at the bottom of the box, so your cat can cover their mess. Place them inside the box for a few minutes each day so they become used to the smell and texture of the litter. Don't be discouraged if they don't relieve themselves right away. You may have to repeat the process several times a day until they finally get the hang of it.

Use the clicker once they're done and present them with a reward. Repeat the same process over the next few days. If you find your cat going to the bathroom somewhere else, interrupt them and place them in the box. Make sure to reward good behavior with heaps of praise and delectable treats.

Remember, accidents are inevitable. Keep an enzymatic cleaner on hand to get rid of the smell and continue the training process. While each cat is unique, most master litter box training in 4 - 6 weeks. If your cat adamantly refuses to use the tray, it could be because of the location. Try placing it in another spot and see if that makes a difference.

Sometimes reluctance to learn litter box training could be a sign of health issues. In such cases, it's best to get your pet examined by a professional and follow their advice.

Deodorizing the Litter Box

Your cat's sensitive nose can turn her into a picky litter connoisseur. A stinky box might send her hunting for an alternate potty spot, leaving you with a mess to clean. Keep both you and your feline friend content by ensuring her bathroom is top-notch.

Show the litter box some love every two to three weeks and give it a deep clean. Grab a metal paint scraper to scrape off the stubborn bits stuck at the bottom. Got more than one cat sharing the same box? You may want to tidy it up more frequently.

Give the container a good shower with hot water and a scrub brush. Make sure there's no litter residue left behind. Mix up a sanitizing solution of 1 teaspoon of household bleach per gallon of hot water. Dip the container for five-minutes in this solution. Rinse it thoroughly and pat dry with paper towels. Sprinkle a pinch of baking soda at the bottom of the box. The odor-absorbing superhero will keep things smelling fresh or opt for a store-bought litter box deodorizer.

Once you're done cleaning, fill it up with a 2-inch layer of non-scented, clumping litter that keeps unwanted smells under wraps. Pour gently to avoid a dust cloud. Always remember the golden rule of washing your hands with antibacterial soap and water post-litter box cleanup to avoid the spread of germs.

Become a daily litter detective! Scoop out the dirties and any kitty gifts at least once a day. More cats mean more scooping! Toss in fresh litter to keep that 2-inch layer intact. And remember, handwashing is a must after attending to litter duties!

Dealing With Cat Toilet Troubles

Around 10% of cats face tricky bathroom issues. Some become box rebels, others prefer using the litter for either urination or defecation, but never both. Some even mix it up, going in the litter, indoors and out. These problems usually arise due to turf wars within the home, litter-box gripes, medical issues, or a simple dislike for box locations.

Once a cat abandons their box, eliminating elsewhere in the house can become a recurring habit. Before you know it, your living room rug is their new bathroom! The key? Prevent this fiasco by keeping an eagle eye on the litter box and your furball's bathroom routine; spotting issues early is the game-changer. If there's a bathroom rebellion, quick action is your best buddy! Resolve it before your cat picks a permanent spot for their private business—trust me, you don't want that!

Cat litter woes are challenging, but a few clever tricks and tricks can help put an end to these messy situations. Here are some reasons that could help you get to the root of the problem and discover the fix for a peaceful litter life with your whiskered buddy.

What's Causing Your Cat to Go "Out of the Box"

Litter-box issues can turn your cat into an amateur interior decorator, but not in the way you'd want! If your furry friend isn't thrilled with their bathroom setup, they might look elsewhere for relief. Messy boxes could be one of the reasons for your cat to ditch the litter for your pristine bedroom carpet. If your cleaning game isn't on point, your cat might protest by skipping the litter box scene.

Space crunch or not having enough litter boxes for all your cats could also make them give up on the litter box entirely. Cats are particular! Provide a box per cat, plus an extra—no sharing allowed. If the box is too tiny, your cat may protest by not using it altogether. Make sure the box is big enough to accommodate your kitty with plenty of room for it to move around while doing its business.

No matter how perfect the litter box is, accessibility is key! If your cat can't access it easily, then it'll show little interest in using it. Get rid of any hoods or liners, if your cat seems to find them bothersome. We discussed cats' high standards when it comes to litter box cleanliness and odor, so make sure the litter is clean and smelling fresh. Another reason your finicky feline may not enjoy using the box could be due to surface preference. Experiment with different types of litter to find the right texture.

If your cat continues avoiding the litter after you've taken care of each minor detail, then it could be due to a traumatic event it may have experienced in the box. Painful eliminations because of constipation could leave a lasting impression on your cat and it may associate the litter box with the pain.

Sudden changes to your cat's daily routine could also result in litter box disruptions. Toilet troubles are bound to spring up when cats feel stressed. Keep your cat's anxiety in check and you won't have to worry about clean ups on your carpet. Household squabbles can be another reason for your cat to suddenly stop heading to the litter box. One cat calling the shots at the litter box can stress out others, leading to a loo rebellion.

Some medical issues that could lead to this problem include urinary tract infections, feline interstitial cystitis, and kidney stones. Urinary Tract Infection could be the culprit if your cat's box visits yield only small dribbles. Feline interstitial cystitis is a complex neurological issue leading to bladder inflammation. Cats with this condition strain while attempting to urinate, often with little success. They may even have blood in their urine and fuss around where they go.

Feline interstitial cystitis could drive them to eliminate outside the box due to urgency and pain. Urgent vet care is vital as it can be a serious and potentially life-threatening illness. Lastly, kidney stones or a blockage bring discomfort and frequent litter box trips for your cat. Look out for signs like vocalizing pain while eliminating or tenderness in the abdomen. Immediate vet attention is crucial.

Resolving Litter Box Problems

The first step in tackling those out-the-box bathroom excursions is ruling out spraying and medical issues. We will discuss spraying (a common territorial trait in cats) in more detail in Chapter 5. Meanwhile, a thorough check by a vet is crucial. Once the doc gives the all-clear, you can start focusing on other issues that may be the culprit.

Start by ensuring there's a box for every furry resident, plus an extra! For three cats, aim for four litter stations. Take the location into account and choose low traffic areas where your kitty won't feel cornered. In multi-level homes, each floor might need a box. Keep boxes away from noisy or intimidating spots, like laundry areas or the dog's chow zone.

Keep food bowls in a separate place from the litter box. Ditch the lids and liners from all boxes. Offer a litter buffet! Clumping, medium-fine texture, unscented—the feline favorite. Set different types side by side and let your cat pick her preferred potty material.

Daily scoop duty is a must. Weekly, give boxes a full scrub with mild, unscented soap or just warm water and replace the litter entirely. Avoid strong scents; they might deter your cat. Remember, accidents happen! Neutralize odors with enzymatic cleansers, found at pet stores. For repeat spots, place litter boxes there.

Surface Preference

Does your cat keep lurking near your favorite rug or keeps darting toward a particular corner in the room to do its business? When your feline friend develops an obvious preference for a specific spot or surface for potty time, it's time to make those places less appealing. Brighten dark corners with motion-activated lights or a bright floor lamp. You can also deter your cat by using upside-down carpet runners, tin foil, or double-sided sticky tape in those areas.

Meanwhile, set up extra litter boxes in acceptable spots and offer various types of litter to see which one she fancies. Line up different litter boxes, each with a different litter type, and let her show you her preference.

Litter Aversion

Cats are creatures of habit, and usually develop their litter preference as kittens. They might have strong opinions about the texture and scent of their litter. While some may adapt to change easily. Others are likely to protest by not using the box at all. Introduce them to different litter types to find what suits them best.

Clumping litter with a medium-fine texture and no scent may work for cats used to going outside. Set up multiple litter boxes with various types of litter, and let them pick their favorite.

Negative Associations

Experiencing a frightening incident in her litter box might make your cat avoid it. This could include loud noises or feeling trapped. For instance, if your cat is cornered while in the litter box by a dog or a person, or startled by a commotion, it may develop litter box aversion.

In some cases, you may even notice your cat going next to the box and not inside it. Another reason to suspect a traumatic incident is responsible for your cat's litter box aversion is if you see your cat running toward the litter box and leaving quickly, sometimes before it's even finished eliminating.

It's important to deal with such situations with the utmost calm and lots of patience. Scolding or manhandling your cat when it goes somewhere else as that will only make them more frightened. Clean accidents thoroughly and consider a new, more private location for the box to prevent surprises.

If your cat reliably used the litter box for elimination in the past, there's a good chance it'll go back to using it without any problems. Observe your cat and think of any possible reasons for the fear. After removing the potential threats, reintroduce your cat to the litterbox. You'll have to be extremely patient as you help your cat recover and reclaim its toilet.

You'll have to go back to square one of litter training and patiently guide your cat to the box after meal times. Stay with it as it does its business at least for a few days until it starts feeling confident again. Reward your cat when it uses the box on its own.

The Takeaway

Successful cat litter box training involves meticulous preparation with the right supplies and an understanding of different litter types and box variations. Consistent training, including placing the cat inside the box regularly and using positive reinforcement like treats, is crucial. However, if initial attempts fail, flexibility is key—try repositioning the box to find the most favorable location. Remember, patience and persistence are fundamental in helping your cat adapt to using the litter box effectively.

If for some reason your cat abruptly stops using the litter box after successful training, there are several ways to overcome this setback. Your cat may need a refresher course but only after you've taken care to remove possible causes behind the litter box rebellion. Try out different kinds of litter, experiment with different container types, change the location, keep the litter box clean and smelling nice and make sure to get rid of distractions.

Make sure the box is placed in an area where your cat doesn't feel trapped and resume training. If your cat chooses a particular area around the house as its toilet spot, preferring it over the litter box, make the area less appealing by installing a bright light or using sticky tape. Restoring your cat's confidence might take time, but slowly and steadily you can help your cat recover.

5

Behavior Modification

"As anyone who has ever been around a cat for any length of time well knows, cats have enormous patience with the limitations of humankind."
– Cleveland Amory

Why is your adorable munchkin dead set on tearing down the house? Why do they keep chewing on your favorite pair of Nikes? How can you get them to stop ripping the upholstery? And what's up with those midnight meowing marathons? If you find yourself at the end of your rope, don't despair. In this chapter, we'll look at some common behavioral problems and ways to overcome them.

Cats are smart creatures with great memories. Experts believe they possess both long-term and short-term memory, making them easy to train. However, this also means they learn which misbehaviors they can get away with based on your response.

Since they remember being rewarded for their actions, you can encourage them to unlearn destructive behavior. Something as simple as a treat, a toy, or a cuddle can work wonders in taming your ferocious furball.

As I mentioned in the previous chapter, you can make rewards more impactful by reserving some goodies solely for training. These could include food items such as tuna, shrimp, canned spray cheese, and catnip toys.

Now let's look at the most troublesome cat habits and what you can do to prevent them.

Scratching Furniture

What beef does your cat have with your sofa or your drapes? Why does it keep attacking them any chance it gets? Contrary to what it may look like, your cat is not on a mission to wreck your house. They're simply acting on their natural instincts. In other words, cats can't help but be cats!

Scratching is primarily a marking behavior that transfers scent from your cat's paws to the sofa or curtain they'd shredded to threads. It stems from an innate urge to mark their territory. This might make it slightly difficult to stop; however, if there's one thing we've learned so far it is that we must never underestimate the power of food over your furry friend. Here are the steps you need to take to put a stop to scratching once and for all:

Identify Your Cat's Favorite Spots

Where does your cat slink off to when it feels the urge to scratch? Does it creep up to the couch, the carpet, or some other surface? Once you've noted what they like, you can think of alternatives. A scratching post with the same material as your carpet or something that offers their claws more resistance could motivate them to give up their favorite spot.

Offer Alternatives That Match Your Cat's Preferences

Depending on what they like, cats will have a varied response to different scratching posts. A cat that prefers running its claws across the couch may prefer nubby surfaces such as sisal or other rope-like material. A cat that perches atop your window sill to attack the curtains, may appreciate a tall post with a long stretch. A cat obsessed with your carpet may take to a flattened scratching board more than the vertical varieties.

If you're a DIY enthusiast, you could build your own scratching posts and activity centers for your cat by fastening bits of carpet, sisal, or fabric to pieces of wood. You can even join these together to construct cat trees. It's important to build a stable structure that won't topple over, posing risks to your cat's safety. This will provide your whiskered warrior ample opportunity to claw away without damaging your precious home decor.

Place the scratching post or cat tree that you've built or purchased near the object that's been the target of your kitty's sharp claws. Whenever you see your tiny furball lurking near the sofa or the curtain, pick them up and place them on the cat tree or scratching post. As I mentioned in Chapter 1, if you're dealing with a particularly stubborn cat, you can try sprinkling catnip on the structure to persuade them.

Eliminate the Satisfaction Factor

The most effective way to put a stop to the mayhem is to take away the satisfaction your cat derives from ruining your treasured carpet or beloved couch. If restricting access to the area is not possible, you can try setting up booby traps to deter them. These could be something as simple as a tower of plastic cups that crash to the floor, startling your sneaky feline.

Double-sided tape or aluminum foil can offer simple yet effective solutions to deter your cat. Use museum putty to stick crumpled pieces of foil along the edges of the couch or apply double sided tape on the corners your cat's most likely to scratch. You can also use slip covers and plastic shields for the corners to prevent damage.

Since cats scratch material they can get a good grip on, you can use plastic sheets to cover your couch as you train them to give up the habit. Because the aim of scratching is to leave their scent and mark their territory, cats return to the same spot to scratch again. Deodorizing these areas could help break the pattern. Make sure to keep positive alternatives such as a cat tree or scratching post nearby, so your dejected cat can find joy using items designed specifically to satisfy its feline instincts.

Clip Those Claws

Another way to minimize future scratching damage is by keeping your cat's nails trimmed. You can also glue plastic nail caps with blunt edges over your cat's claws to protect your furniture during the training process.

You'll need your cat to sit patiently while you slip on the caps, so some level of obedience is required to try out this method. Moreover, the caps need to be replaced every 6 to 12 weeks. With this method, you don't have to keep a constant eye on your cat or worry about your couch being reduced to shreds.

Punishment Is Counterproductive

Cats are incapable of forming a link between punitive measures and their actions. So any form of punishment to discipline them is bound to backfire and may even lead to more aggression. Some disciplinary methods that you should avoid at all costs include yelling, startling them with a loud noise, or squirting them with water.

At best, punishments only teach the cat not to perform certain actions when their owner is around rather than bringing about lifelong changes. Setting up deterrents is more effective at discouraging negative behaviors without compromising your relationship with your pet.

Chewing On Fabric

My rollercoaster experience of training Kiki made me believe I'd seen it all. Then came Zoe and Charlie and I was instantly humbled. My Burmese and Siamese cats had a strange tendency for chewing on my sweaters, socks, and blankets! I set out to investigate why they felt compelled to damage my wardrobe and was relieved to learn it wasn't because of my fashion sense.

While fabric chewing is relatively rare in cats, it is a comfort-seeking behavior commonly observed in Burmese and Siamese breeds. Most kittens are also prone to munching on soft, woolen blankets or socks, although they usually outgrow the habit. Wool is the fabric of choice in most cases, with pillows, sweaters, and blankets becoming common targets.

In addition to damaging your bedding and clothes, your cat can end up harming its own health by ingesting cloth fibers. The habit can also lead to an increased risk of choking or swallowing small sharp objects such as pins or needles.

Prevention Is Better Than Cure

As we discussed previously, restricting access to potentially dangerous or valuable items is usually the quickest and most inexpensive solution. You can also offer your cat rubber toys scented with fish oil to munch on as an alternative. So lock your closet and keep those expensive sweaters out of reach.

Beat the Boredom

Cats that habitually chew on household objects may just be bored. Cat condos offering numerous crawl spaces and perches could keep them busy and entertained for a long time. You can create games to distract your cat from destructive urges. Simply hanging a toy on top of them, dangling ribbons, or tossing ping pong balls or walnuts for them to fetch could be a fun pastime.

Cat Repellent Sprays

Spray pet repellents on the items your cat loves feasting on to make them less appetizing. Use it periodically on multiple items so your cat learns all fabrics taste bad. As cats tend to be more sensitive to strong scents, such as lavender and citrus, these can be used to repel them. Substitutes that can be used for lemon, orange, and lavender include lime, peppermint, and eucalyptus. If you're on a budget and possess a creative streak, you can whip up your own repellent spray with the following recipes:

Essential Oil Mixture

Lemon essential oil	2 drops
Lavender essential oil	2 drops
Water	

Vinegar Mixture

Vinegar	1 part
Liquid hand soap	1 part
Water	1 part

Citrus Spray

Water	2 cups (473 ml)
Citrus fruit peels	1 cup (96 g)
Lemon scented dish soap	

Garlic, Pepper, and Lemon Spray

Black pepper	1 teaspoon (2 g)
Dry mustard	1 teaspoon (2 g)
Cinnamon	1 teaspoon (2 g)
Garlic clove	1 crushed
Lemon essential oil	3 to 4 drops
Water	

Make sure to store essential oil mixtures in glass bottles because they tend to degrade in plastic containers. You can use the repellents above to prevent your cat from nibbling on your plants, scratching furniture, and damaging outdoor garden beds.

Medical Intervention

Certified animal behaviorist Mikel Delgado says that frequently chewing on fabrics could be a sign of a condition called pica. "If the cat is actually eating parts of the fabric or other objects, it can cause digestive problems," Delgado says. "It also can cause an impaction, so it could require surgery."

She emphasizes the importance of getting your cat examined by a vet as soon as possible to rule out medical problems (Greene, 2018). Stress plays a huge role in causing pica or compulsive behavior due to anxiety. However, it could also be a sign of a much deeper problem such as gastrointestinal or digestive issues.

Marking Territory With A Tinkle

I remember watching Kiki with awe as she prowled around the house one day. She strutted down the hallway, exuding a majestic aura, stopped near the staircase, lifted her hindleg, and....!

What just happened? She'd mastered using the litterbox months ago. So why did she tinkle on the runner? I felt stumped.

Spraying is more commonly observed in male, unneutered cats. A possible trigger for this behavior is anxiety caused by changes in schedule, environment, or family such as a marriage, divorce, new baby, or new cat. Strong visual, olfactory, or auditory stimuli could also be a triggering factor.

Fix the Problem

Observe your cat and note the places it marks. Usually, when marking their territory, cats lift their tail and spray a small amount instead of crouching down the way they would in a litter box.

Put extra litter boxes on these spots and clean soiled litter more frequently. Disinfect marked areas with antibacterial or enzymatic cleaners. Finally, address the underlying causes to put a stop to the habit for good. In some cases, the vet may prescribe medication to curb the behavior.

Getting your cat neutered can solve the problem sometimes, although 10% of neutered cats continue to exhibit the same behavior. Identifying the trigger for the problem is the first step.

Increasing playtime with your kitty can also bring down their stress levels.

Excessive spraying could also be due to territorial disputes between cats living in the same house. Try separating them from each other and confining them to their own safe areas. Lastly, use odor neutralizers like Feliway, an artificial pheromone that mimics cat's scent and may significantly reduce spraying.

Aggression Toward Strangers and Other Cats

Cats that bite or lash out during play could have a low tolerance for physical contact. Some may bite people to stop them from approaching and touching them while they're resting or eating. Likewise, they may show increased aggression to a stranger approaching them when they're frightened or anxious.

Cats are notoriously jealous of other felines in the same household, especially when they're introduced to each other. Usually, their fury stems from the desire to protect their sleeping areas and other possessions. Baring of the teeth or a growl toward an unfamiliar cat is mostly due to fear and has a territorial element to it.

De-Escalate and Desist

If your cats are in the middle of a fight, break up the brawl and separate them to prevent injuries. Restrict them to different areas until they've calmed down. If you notice that fights usually break out at a specific time during the day, separate the cats at those times to prevent conflict.

The scent of the other cats is usually the trigger for aggression, so desensitization or counterconditioning could minimize violent outbursts. You can do this by using the same grooming tools or gradually bringing the cats closer to one another by allowing them to eat in the same area.

Giving them access to more three dimensional structures such as cat trees could keep them out of each other's way. You can train one or both cats with a leash or a harness to keep them at a safe distance from each other. If one cat is usually the aggressor, tying a bell around their neck could help alert the victim about their whereabouts and run for cover. Make sure to reward the cats for their positive interactions with others and continue the training practice.

Dealing With Feline Compulsive Disorders

Odd, repetitive behaviors in cats could be a sign of a compulsive disorder. They're usually intensified versions of normal behaviors such as stalking, grooming, or chasing exacerbated by anxiety and stress. Examples of these behaviors include excessive grooming, causing self-injury, biting, sucking, or chewing non-nutritive objects.

If the condition persists or worsens with time, you may want to get your cat looked at by an expert to ascertain whether they're suffering from compulsive disorders. The medicines prescribed following a positive diagnosis can help alleviate the symptoms of this disorder considerably.

Excessive Vocalizations

Kiki's musical ambitions caught me by surprise. As supportive as I wanted to be of her midnight practice sessions, the constant sleep deprivation made it impossible to cheer her on when she belted out those high notes.

Cats communicate with each other through a variety of different sounds such as meowing, hissing, and purring. Some cat breeds, like the Siamese, make more noise than others. Usually, vocalization increases during mating season, so getting your cat neutered may solve the problem.

Excessive meowing could also be a sign of distress. Moving to a new home or being confined inside the house for a long time could be some possible triggers. This is why it's important to determine the cause of your cat's increased vocalization. If medical issues are ruled out then it could be because your cat wants you to attend to their needs such as feeding them or taking them outside.

Boredom could also be one of the reasons. Mentally and physically stimulating activities could help solve the problem. To prevent nighttime solo concerts, schedule playtime close to bedtime followed by a protein rich dinner to satisfy their hunting instincts. This routine is most likely to curb meowing sessions later in the night.

If the above trick is unsuccessful, you could try leaving out a food puzzle to keep your cat's brain occupied and tummy full when it does wake up in the night. If your cat still continues to make a lot of noise even when you've provided them with the proper nourishment and medical issues have been ruled out then it's best to ignore them. The more often you give your cat what it wants after it's made a lot of racket, the more your cat learns to repeat the behavior. Eventually, they'll assume that it's the only reliable way to grab your attention.

Respond to them when they quiet down. Initially, when you begin ignoring them, they're more likely to make more noise for longer durations before finally giving up. It's important to remain steadfast to see results. Giving in when your cat intensifies its vocalization only gives the message that they need to meow longer and louder for you to finally do their bidding. While ignoring attention seeking behavior, don't forget to reward positive actions. When your cat quietly approaches you, attend to their needs and give them a treat.

The Takeaway

Keeping a cat as a pet isn't always a walk in the park. However, most problems can be overcome through positive reinforcement and a few clever tricks. Damaging furniture is usually cat owners' top concern. Identifying the places your cat prefers to scratch is the first step toward solving this problem. Once you've singled out the objects, you can limit access and protect those areas while providing alternatives.

Problems such as chewing on fabrics, spraying, compulsive disorders, bouts of aggression, and excessive vocalizations can be dealt with in a similar manner. You can trust your tiny furball to test your patience sometimes. Effective training techniques improve your relationship with your pet while bringing a stop to stress-causing behavior. It's not always going to be sunshine and rainbows, but the cuddles and purrs make it all worth it!

6

More Tricks to Keep Them Busy!

"Cats are inquisitive, but hate to admit it."
– Mason Cooley

Once you've covered the basics, it's time to level up and teach some advanced tricks. Clicker training and using the target stick lie at the heart of most tricks, so you need your cat to master this skill. Having overcome problems associated with basic obedience training, teaching additional tricks may seem like a hassle. However, the multitude of advantages of teaching your pet more skills make it worthwhile.

Learning more tricks helps animals build more muscles, and improves flexibility, concentration, and balance. It boosts your pet's confidence and strengthens trust between them and their owner. It can be a great bonding experience between you and your cat as well as an excellent source of entertainment.

Here are some fun tricks you can teach your kitty:

Speak

This is a simple, cute trick to get your cat to converse with you. Hold up a toy and say "Speak." As soon as your cat meows to ask for it, give them the toy and a treat. You'll be surprised when they change the pitch and tone of their meows based on what they're trying to tell you. This will also teach your cat not to make too much noise when it wants something and minimize excessive vocalizations. It'll keep them engaged for a long time while helping reduce other undesired behaviors.

Jump Into Your Arms

You're getting late and you can't get a hold of your fluffy feline! Just when you try to catch them and shove them inside their carrier, they race out of your reach. Wouldn't it be great if your cat leapt into your arms when you wanted them to? It may seem like a dream, especially when you're dealing with a hyperactive pet.

It may take some time for your cat to learn this trick. You'll have to build it up slowly. Start by sitting on a chair and using the clicker to get your cat to jump into your lap. Use the command "Jump" as you encourage them to rush into your arms. Close your arms around them after the first few attempts.

Make sure to give rewards when they get it right. Once they've mastered running into your arms when you're sitting, try to get them to jump up while you stand. When they start responding to this command, you can take it up a notch and teach more tricks such as jumping through a hula hoop or over an object.

Jump through Hoop

Ever seen a circus lion jumping through hoops? Your cat can do it too! All you need is a hula hoop and a cat that's up to learning some new tricks. Hold the hula hoop before your cat. Crouch down and hold a treat in your hand on the other side of the hoop. Use the command "Come" to encourage your cat to walk through it.

The next step is to hold the hoop a little above the floor. Use the command "Jump" to urge your cat to jump through the hoop. If you've got a particularly athletic and agile cat, you can lift the hoop a little higher to make this trick even more impressive!

High Five

One of my favorite tricks to teach my cats and an absolute classic is the high five. Get a cup of treats ready. Hold it up so your cat paws at the cup. Gradually, remove the cup and hold the treat in your hand. If they try to get it with their mouth, clench your fist. You can also hold the treat by making a cup shape with your hand, so your cat can only reach it with its paw.

As soon as they get the treat out, say "High five." With the treat wedged between your fingers, hold your hand up vertically. Once your cat begins associating the command "High five" with the action of placing its paw on your hand, you can stop using the treat. Present them with a reward whenever they tap your palm after listening to the command.

Freeze dried treats are usually the healthiest option for this trick and will fit easily in your hand. Level up by teaching your cat to fist bump. Follow the same steps as before, simply changing the shape and positioning of your hand.

Figure of Eight

Teach your cat to make a figure of eight around your legs or around an object. All you need is your target wand. Use the wand to encourage them to make a figure of eight around your legs and reward them when they get it right.

Fetch

Roll a toy a foot away from you. Use the target stick to prompt your cat to go after it. The moment it picks up the toy, use the clicker and give them a treat. Repeat the process until your cat associates picking up the toy with the reward. They may not walk back to you with the toy in their mouth right away. Break the trick into small achievable goals.

For example, reward them if they turn to look at you with the toy in their mouth. After a few successful attempts, delay the reward in order to encourage them to take a few steps toward you. Gradually, with lots of practice, they'll learn to bring the toy to you. Place your hand under their mouth to urge them to drop the toy in it. Use the clicker and reward them whenever they do so.

If chasing after toys doesn't come to your cat naturally, you can start by giving them an item containing a treat. The snack will encourage them to pick the toy from the ground. I prefer small webbed or woven balls designed for holding pet treats. You can find plastic versions of these toys, but cats may have some difficulty lifting them with their mouth and getting to the treat.

Once you've placed the treat inside the webbing, show it to your cat. If they show even mild interest in the toy or give it a sniff, mark it with a click and give them a treat. Repeat this a few times then hold off the reward and bring their attention to the treat inside the ball. When they start playing with the ball without your encouragement, you can remove the treat and follow the steps above to teach them to fetch.

You'll need to be extra patient with this trick as you slowly build your cat's skills. Remember, practice makes perfect, so keep going even when you don't see visible progress. You certainly won't regret it!

Spin

Most cats learn this trick fairly quickly, but some may require a little practice. Hold up your cat's favorite treat and slowly move it in a horizontal circle. Make sure to hold it up to eye level with your cat and move your hand slowly while saying "Spin." If you go too fast, your cat may stop and spin the other way. When they complete one spin, toss the treat at them as a reward.

When it seems like your cat's got a hang of it, you can start holding the treat further away while asking them to spin. The goal is for them to learn to follow your command without the treat in sight. Keep practicing until they learn to spin on your verbal instruction and a simple hand gesture.

Roll Over

This may be the easiest trick you'll come across! Simply sit beside your cat while it's lying down and hold a treat an inch or two away from its nose. Say "Roll over" while moving your hand in an arc. This will prompt your cat to tilt its head and roll over to its side to sniff and grab the treat. Break the method into small steps, if your cat refuses to budge. Reward them as they tilt their head then delay the reward until they roll over.

Wear A Leash

With a leash and harness, your furry friend can safely accompany you on your morning walks. The first thing you'll need is a leash and harness that meets your cat won't want to squirm out of. Use the points given in Chapter 2 to find a perfect match. Once you've got your hands on a good leash or harness, let your cat play with it a bit. This will make them feel comfortable and get cozy with it.

Practice putting it on and taking it off, treating them like royalty the whole time. Once the harness is on, clip on the leash and use more treats to encourage normal walking. When they seem comfortable with that, take them outside to explore a secure spot. Reward every step of the way. Gradually, increase the amount of time they're on the leash by strolling in a bigger area.

Remember, it's not like walking a dog. Your cat will need some time to get used to it. Let them explore their surroundings and even do some rolling around. You're on the right track as long as they seem to be enjoying themselves. Eventually, slipping on the harness and clipping on the leash will feel natural to them.

The Takeaway

Mastering these advanced tricks can truly deepen the bond between you and your feline companion. Through patience, dedication, and a shared sense of fun, you can unlock a whole new level of communication and understanding with your cat. From jumping through a hoop to mastering playing fetch and spinning around with finesse, there's a lot that you can teach.

Each learned trick represents not just their capabilities but also the strong connection and trust between them and their owner. As you continue this journey of learning and fun, remember, it's not just about the tricks; it's about the moments of joy that these activities foster between you and your remarkable feline friend.

7

Cat Training for Special Cases

"How we behave toward cats here below determines
our status in heaven."

– Robert A. Heinlein

You can't teach an old dog new tricks, but what about cats? Is training a senior cat even possible? Can your cat recover from anxiety? Should you go ahead with training them?

The answer to the above questions is a resounding yes!

Maybe you've adopted an older cat or you're looking for ways to engage your elderly pet in fun activities. Maybe you want them to get some exercise and shed a few pounds. Regardless of your reasons, training senior cats and cats with medical problems is not only possible but a necessity.

But before we jump into the ins and outs of training senior cats, let's look at cat age and what's considered "old." Six months old or younger are identified as kittens while adolescents are six months to two years old. Between two and ten years is the adult stage of the feline lifecycle while any cat whose age is ten years or more is considered old.

Like humans, aging in cats doesn't follow a strict timeline. Depending on their lifestyle and diet, some cats may show signs of aging earlier or later than others. Other influencing factors include environment, genetics, mental well-being, and veterinary care. So without further ado, here are some tips to help train cats with special needs.

Training Senior Cats

Delectable treats remain the strongest motivator for cats of all ages. Freeze-dried chicken or fresh tuna is a great way to capture your elderly cat's attention and get them to move. Just make sure to keep the bites small as weight gain can further decrease mobility in older cats. The next thing you need is your trusted clicker device, which is just as effective on senior cats as it is on jumpy kittens.

Remember to set your cat up for success by starting small. Gradually work your way up from the basics to slightly more complicated tricks such as high five or playing fetch. Set reasonable expectations and celebrate small achievements. Slowly but surely, your cat will learn all the tricks you've lined up.

Focusing on the basics at the onset also prevents boredom or frustration. With your spirits up, you remain committed to reaching the finish line. Keeping it simple means having more fun and bonding with your cat. Most of your success with senior cats depends on patience and positive reinforcement, so stress-free training sessions and an extra bag of your cat's favorite treats are your best bet.

Recall Training

Recall training is especially useful for elderly felines. This includes teaching them to respond to their name being called. For senior cats, this simple trick could be potentially lifesaving. Should they ever get lost, you'll have a better chance of finding them if they're trained to come to you.

As with other cats, the best time to train is just before mealtimes when they'll appreciate the treats more. Call out your cat's name followed by the cue "Come." Start by training inside the house at first. Increase the distance between yourself and your cat gradually. Move to an adjacent room and repeat the cue.

On average, it should take about 10 - 20 daily sessions for a week or so for your whiskered friend to master this trick.

Leash Training

Older kitties need plenty of exercise to burn that extra fat and stay healthy. Daily strolls around the neighborhood not only boost your cat's physical health, but improve their mental well-being as well. Cats are natural explorers, so creating a safe environment for them to follow their instincts is a must.

Leash training older cats follows the same steps. Get a harness that's a comfortable fit for your cat. Keep it near your cat's favorite spot for a few days so they get used to it. Put the harness on your cat and reward them for not kicking up a fuss. Let them wear it for a few hours each day. Offer rewards to keep them motivated. When they stop resisting, it's time to clip on the leash and take them outdoors.

It's important to keep the transition process deliberately slow to build up your cat's comfort level. When you finally take them outside, shower them with treats for successfully covering short distances. If they don't seem too keen on walking with a leash, you can lay treats in their path to encourage them to follow you.

Litter Box Training

In Chapter 4, we briefly discussed some factors you must keep in mind when choosing a litter box for a senior cat. Litter training older cats may present a few problems especially if they failed to learn to use the litter box as kittens. Even if your cat mastered going to the toilet when it was young, elimination problems may appear during old age. Take a proactive approach by looking out for the warning signs.

Health Alarm Bells

Litter problems in elderly cats may arise due to changes in schedule and environment or medical issues. For example, a sudden change in your cat's elimination habits could be due to illness, making a veterinary examination a top priority. Hyperthyroidism, lower urinary tract infections, diabetes and kidney disease are fairly common in older cats. Other conditions that may cause litterbox dysfunction include arthritis, degenerative joint disease or spinal problems.

Relieving itself or climbing into the litter box may be painful for your cat in the above conditions. It may begin associating the pain with the litter box and relieve itself somewhere else to reduce its discomfort.

Giving up on the litter box could also be due to decreased vision, glaucoma or blindness. Usually, blind cats memorize important locations such as their food bowl and the litter box. In such cases, you may not notice a change in their behavior until you move around the furniture.

Feline cognitive dysfunction (CFD) marks cognitive decline in cats including symptoms such as deteriorating memory, hearing, sight, and learning ability. Cats exhibiting symptoms of dementia may simply forget the location of their litter box. If the diagnosis comes out to be positive, the vet may prescribe supplements or medication to help alleviate the symptoms.

Helping Older Cats Overcome Litter Box Problems

All this may paint a gloomy picture for old cats suffering with medical issues, but it's important to remember there are numerous ways for you to ease their discomfort. The bond between you and your pet deepens with time, so it makes sense to look out for your feline friend when they're most vulnerable. Here are some ways to help your older cat overcome litter box problems:

- **Maintain a consistent daily routine.** Elderly cats in particular don't respond well to sudden changes in their schedule or their environment. Abrupt changes in their routine may lead to increased anxiety, cognitive decline, and litter box problems.
- **Keep the litter box in the same place.** If it's absolutely necessary for you to move it, then leave a recent deposit in it, so your cat can trace it by scent. Help your cat find and remember the new location. You can also place puppy pads around the box, if it seems that your cat has trouble getting inside.
- **Keep it clean and secluded.** Cats are neat freaks by nature and value privacy. With advancing age, they may become less patient and more finicky. So, while a less-than-perfect litter box may have flown under the radar of an adult cat, your older feline may snub it altogether. Instead, you'd find her seeking out other places around the house for an undisturbed toilet session. This is your cue to keep the litter box immaculate, accessible, and in a quiet area away from your cat's bed and food bowl.

- **Add another one.** Bladder retention decreases with age, making it difficult for old furries to hold it in long enough. Accidents may happen as they rush across the house or climb the stairs to get to their litter box. Make things easier for your elderly cat by providing a litter box on each floor.

- **Adjust the size of the box.** Regular litter boxes may be difficult for arthritic cats to climb who may prefer one with low sides. You can create your own from a plastic box or storage container or cut down the sides of their old litter box. Discarded aluminum bakeware that is the same size as a roasting pan can also be a great option. If you still have to modify the sides, make sure not to leave any sharp edges. You can also skip the hassle, and simply add a ramp to your litter box setup.

- **Change the litter.** Adjust the amount of litter inside. A large volume could create an unbalanced surface, making it difficult for an elderly cat to squat. Clumping litters with fine-grain texture are usually the best choice for older cats. Strong smells might be off-putting for senior felines, so opt for unscented varieties.

Dealing with Untrained Cats

A few years ago, a friend of mine took in an elderly cat from a relative. She instantly fell in love with the white ragdoll. However, to her dismay, she soon discovered it hadn't been litter trained. The previous owner simply let the cat go wherever it wanted and cleaned up later. Determined not to give up on him, she used different tactics to get him trained. From scattering pads across the house to buying litter boxes of all kinds (open, closed, self-cleaning, you name it!), but, Snowball, the elderly ragdoll, showed zero interest.

Just when she was about to lose hope, she contacted me. Together, we devised a roadmap to help the elderly feline learn toilet etiquettes. Since an untrained cat may view the entire house as a one big litter box, we had to implement the confinement method to get the wizened cat litter trained.

Here are the steps to create a cozy confined space for your cat while it undergoes seclusion training:

Step 1

Get your hands on a large pet crate and place it in a quiet area in the laundry room or the bathroom. Place a large litter box at the rear of the crate to give your cat some privacy.

Step 2

Place their food and water bowl in the center of the crate and position the bed or blanket in the front. This way your cat will have a clear view of the house when it rests. Don't forget to add a few of your cat's favorite toys inside for playtime.

Step 3

Once the setup is ready, it's time to put your cat inside their new cozy home. Diligently clean the litter box more than once daily with a litter scoop. Change the litter once a week, wash the box thoroughly with soap, rinse well, and air dry.

Step 4

Once the cat starts using the litter box, move it out of the crate, but keep it confined in the small room for a few days and continue training. Make sure to spend lots of time with your fuzzy friend to keep them calm. Use an enzyme cleaner to clean up any accidents and mask unpleasant smells.

Step 5

Move your cat to a larger room as soon as "accidents" outside the litter box become more infrequent.

Step 6

You're close to the finish line! The confinement method combined with positive reinforcement has worked its magic. It's time to decide the final spot for the litter box in your house. In the unlikely event that your cat returns to eliminating in its favorite spot instead of the litter, simply scoop up the excrement and put it in the litter box. Next, pick up your cat and place it inside, encouraging it to bury the excrement by scooping a bit of litter on it. Present it with a reward when it does so. Continue the practice until your elderly feline is completely trained.

Points to Remember

Old cats lack the capabilities of lively kittens or robust adult cats, making it necessary for you to modify your training methods. Tailor your exercises to match their abilities and maximize their comfort. Keep the sessions short and rule out physically demanding tricks such as jumping through hoops. You can still have lots of fun with your cat as it enters old age in different ways. Your patience and kindness could make all the difference for your elderly pet as it battles cognitive and physical decline. Keep a positive mindset, with the goal of bringing joy to your senior cat.

Anxious Cats

Just as humans, cats experience a range of emotions including anxiety. If left untreated for a prolonged period of time, it can impact their physical and mental health. Cats riddled with anxiety may react fearfully toward new objects or changes in their home environment. While it can be heartbreaking to see your furry friend suffering in this way, there are ways you can help. The first step is identifying the triggers, so if you suspect you're dealing with a particularly anxious pet, it's time to put on your detective hat and get to work.

Warning Signs

Anxiety may bubble to the surface due to underlying health issues, making a detailed examination by the vet a top priority. In some cases, addressing the medical problem may be all that's needed to help your cat recover. Symptoms of anxiety tend to be rather obscure. If these cats went around with their hair puffed up, backs arched and teeth bared, it'd be much easier to make a diagnosis. As it turns out, that's not the case.

Although anxiety shows up in a variety of ways, there are a few key symptoms. Change in daily habits such as an altered sleep schedule, litter box problems, weight fluctuations, and frequent illnesses such as diarrhea or vomiting.

Therefore, if you catch your snooze ball alert during nap times or your bright eyed feline feeling drowsier than usual, it could be a sign that something is awry. Similarly, if the food bowl remains untouched or nothing can bring a stop to your cat's cries for hunger, then it could be due to a bout of anxiety.

Signs of intense fear and anxiety are hard to miss. Rapid breathing, trembling, tail flicking or holding it tightly coiled to their body, dilated pupils, and flattened ears are some indications of danger. Crouching down, hair standing up, avoiding eye contact, and excessive vocalizations such as meowing, growling, hissing, or yowling are your cat's ways of telling you it's not alright. Other signs include compulsively licking their nose, excessive grooming, pacing back and forth, aggression and increased destructive behaviors such as scratching furniture.

You may notice your fiercely independent cat meekly following you around the house and getting startled easily by loud sounds or sudden movement. The appearance of one or two symptoms generally isn't a cause for alarm. Unless you observe multiple signs regularly, you've got nothing to worry about.

Road to Recovery

There's no magic pill to make cat anxiety go away in a day or two. A multi-pronged approach is required to bring about lasting change. As mentioned above, identifying the triggers is the first step. Possible causes of anxiety include changes in your pet's environment such as moving to a new home, repositioning the furniture, introducing a new litter box, addition of a new family member or pet. A traumatic event, illness, or improper care during kittenhood can also lead to onset of anxiety.

Finding out the precise trigger is crucial. Try to think of any recent changes in your home and whether they coincide with changes in your cat's behavior. Observe your cat throughout the day and take note of the time and place where symptoms show up. Record them whenever they display anxiety to help you connect the dots. Once you've pinpointed the cause, you can take steps to remove or minimize the trigger as much as possible.

The best way to manage your cat's anxiety is to make changes in its environment, introduce calming strategies, and vet prescribed anti-anxiety medicine. Recovery may take several months depending on your consistency and commitment. Be patient and remember that every small change counts! Here are some strategies to deal with the different triggers of anxiety in cats:

Tackling the Green Eyed Monster

Seeing another cat in the house made Kiki green with envy. She prowled through the house filled with rage, ready to take a swipe at Zoe any chance she got. Naturally, it made me feel more protective of my new pet. As I showered Zoe with cuddles and presents, Kiki became more and more withdrawn.

Since cats are instinctively territorial, feelings of anxiety naturally kick in when they see an intruder. Here was a strange new cat that had taken over her house and stolen her owner's affection. Expecting Kiki to be polite and gracious toward someone considered an invader was unreasonable.

The only way to assist her in managing her anxiety was ensuring her that she had her own territory and there was no competition for resources. This meant creating a safe space for Kiki away from the trigger: Zoe.

I moved Kiki to a smaller room for a few days where she wouldn't have to deal with the new cat. I made sure she had everything she'd need (food, water, scratching post, toys, and bedding), then it was time to flood her with loads of individual attention, cuddles, and playtime.

If you don't have a spare cubby hole in your house, you can reserve a corner for your cat. Place their cave bed or an upturned basket along with their favorite things and limit access of the other cat to that area for a few days. Cat shelves, window perches, and cat trees can also be used for this purpose.

You can simmer down tensions between the feuding felines by keeping their litter boxes separate. Avoid placing them in an enclosed space where your cat could become trapped if it's attacked by the aggressor. Mealtimes should also be separate to avoid conflict as you help your cats cope with anxiety and aggression.

Coping Strategies

An idle pet, with no outlet to channel its energy, easily succumbs to nerves. Mental stimulation and exercise are prerequisites for happy and healthy cats. Toys and feeder puzzles can keep them entertained. Daily walks, outdoor play, and lots and lots of scratching can help them vent their feelings.

Additionally, you can use natural pheromone sprays to mitigate feline anxiety. Pheromones are chemicals emitted by cats and other animals including humans in response to specific emotions. The pheromones released when these animals are in calm and relaxed state can induce calm in others. Cats pick up on these chemical signals and are able to make better judgments about approaching other animals. This way, they can avoid anxious or territorial felines and have a friendly interaction with a happy cat.

Using pheromone sprays and diffusers is a great way to induce calm in pets suffering from anxiety. You can apply a few spritz on their scratching posts, bedding, and other objects that they interact with frequently or use pheromone-diffusing collars. CBD oil is another great option to calm frayed nerves. However, make sure to consult your vet before using CBD products because while their effectiveness on dogs is undisputed, they're not FDA approved for therapeutic use on cats.

Other techniques include desensitization and counterconditioning. Desensitization involves exposing your cat to the trigger in small doses repeatedly and rewarding positive behavior. For example, if the trigger is the sound of a dog barking, play the sound at a low volume whenever your cat is in a calm state. Increase the volume a little after each successful session until they become accustomed to it. Take care not to overdo it. You don't want to end up causing more stress to your furry friend and exacerbating the problem. Keep an eye out for your cat's body language, especially the positioning of their tail and ears, for any signs of discomfort.

Counter conditioning helps change your cat's response to the trigger through positive reinforcement. If feelings of anxiety surface in your cat when another pet is in the vicinity, feed them their favorite snack every time they see them to build a positive association. Finally, if all else fails, you may have to turn to vet prescribed anti-anxiety medications to get things under control.

Preparing Cats for Special Situations

I was convinced there was nothing Kiki hated more than when the spotlight shifted from her furry mane to someone else. She was the star of the show and anything or anyone who dared challenge her position summoned her inner demons. That was until her first visit to the vet. From that moment on, Kiki kicked up a storm every time she sensed I was taking her to the vet.

It's quite common for cats to be afraid of vets, wreak havoc during travel or freeze in emergency situations. The good news is there are steps you can take to prepare your cat beforehand to make the experience less unpleasant. Let's start with vet visits and what you can do to disarm your feline opponent.

Vet Visits

Whether it's a routine checkup or an emergency appointment, you can make the experience stress free with a few tips. First and foremost, it's important for you to stay calm. Start early so you don't panic about running late. Chasing your cat around the house or yelling at it will only make matters worse.

The calmer you feel, the more likely your cat will stay calm as well. Speak softly with them, gently coaxing it into the carrier. The best way to get a particularly resistant cat into the carrier is to place a treat or toy inside. Remain calm if your cat puts up a fight when it finds itself trapped. Speak to it softly and play gentle music or white noise to soothe its nerves during the drive.

Most cats only get placed inside the carrier when it's time to see the vet. Kiki would catch one glimpse of the carrier and start freaking out. If your cat fusses about going inside the carrier too, leave it out as much as possible. Serve your cat's meals inside, so it stops seeing it as a sign of something awful that's about to happen. Make sure to leave the carrier out for a few days before the vet visit, so its presence doesn't enrage your tiny warrior.

Be generous with the treats especially if it helps your cat feel less nervous. Reward your furry friend for successfully getting inside the carrier, and make sure they have more snacks to nibble on during the ride. However, take care not to overfeed them before placing them in the car or they may get carsick.

If your cat has a favorite pillow, bed, toy, or blanket, bring it along to make them feel better. If cuddling helps your little munchkin calm down, place your old T-shirt in the carrier or hold them in your lap while someone else drives. A little catnip can also help bring your cat's frayed nerves under control.

Moreover, you can further decrease your cat's discomfort about being examined by holding its head and tail and examining it at home. Don't forget to reward your cat for good behavior. If car rides are what send your cat into a frenzy, put your cat in its harness and leash and take it with you to run small errands in your car.

Travel

Traveling with pets is tricky, but sometimes it is unavoidable. If your cat's prone to awful separation anxiety or you simply want them by your side enjoying the island breeze, traveling with your pet doesn't have to be the headache it's usually made out to be. As always, everything depends on preparation.

With some smart prep, you can make traveling with your feline master less daunting. Your globetrotting experience with a cat depends largely on your cat's temperament. While some may prove to be lively travel companions with a flair for adventure, others may only feel safe and comfortable in familiar surroundings.

Hiring a cat sitter, leaving your cat with a friend or a relative are some options you can consider if you don't want your cat tagging along. Buying a pet auto feeder, auto litter cleaner, pet cameras and treat dispensers are some nifty gadgets that you can invest in if you have the budget and plan on leaving your cat home alone. In the instance that taking your cat along with you is the only option available, there's a lot you can do to make the experience worthwhile.

Getting your cat used to being enclosed in the carrier is essential. The steps outlined above as well as the tricks in Chapter 3 are great for helping your cat overcome claustrophobia or anxiety. Secure the carrier with the seatbelt to keep your cat safe during long car rides.

While you're getting your identification and travel documents in order make sure to snap on your cat's collar or ID tag, you can also microchip your cat for extra measure. A collar can slip off, but with a microchip you can track them down no matter what.

Before you hop on the plane with your tiny cat-venturer in tow, make sure to visit the vet. Get them checked for any health conditions that may be brewing inside. Make other arrangements if they seem to be suffering from an illness to help them recover. A drastic change in a cat's environment when it's not in the best of its health could add to its misery and make matters worse.

If your cat is in for a road trip, get it used to long car rides by taking it along for short trips. Start with a brief ten minute drive around the neighborhood, gradually adding five minutes to the ride after each successful attempt. These short trips can also help you uncover problems you may not be aware of in your cat such as hyperactivity or motion sickness.

A hyperactive cat may yowl, salivate, meow, or shake its carrier. A vet prescribed sedative or anti-nausea medication may help solve the problem. In addition to these, you can spray pheromones on the carrier or put on a snug fitting shirt on your cat, which works the same way as a swaddle.

Remember, cats can't be confined in a small space for too long. Make room for short breaks to give your cat the opportunity to stretch its legs, use the litter or have a drink.

For plane rides, make sure to check the airline's policy about traveling with pets. Take note of the allowed size of cat carrier and prepare vaccination records and health certificates from your veterinarian. Leave for the airport earlier to give yourself ample time. Passing through TSA checkpoints may take slightly longer with pets as you get them out of the carrier to pass it through the X-ray machine.

As I mentioned before, preparation is key, and it all starts with making a list of cat essentials. Here are all the items that will come in handy as you travel with your furry pal at your heels:

- Portable food and water bowls
- Cat food
- Treats
- Cat harness and leash
- Pet cleaning product and paper towels for accidents or if your cat gets sick
- First aid kit
- Blanket or towel
- Your cat's favorite toy
- Travel scratching post or a cardboard scratch pad
- A portable litter box and plastic bags to dispose of excrement in case of accidents
- Puppy pads to line the carrier
- Any medication your cat may be taking

Make sure to feed your kitty at least two to three hours before leaving for your trip. Serving your cat a huge meal just before leaving could increase their chances of throwing up or needing to use the litter box during the ride. Once you've ticked all the boxes on your checklist, you'll be good to go. Take a deep breath and set sail for distant shores with your furry feline!

Emergency Situations

Disaster strikes when you least expect it. Preparing for the unexpected could potentially save you and your pet's life. An emergency kit is essential for a quick evacuation. Sadly, pets are usually not taken into account while preparing emergency supplies. As a result, pet parents are caught off-guard during a crisis.

In a recent survey, the American Society for the Prevention of Cruelty to Animals (ASPCA) found that almost half of the one in five animal owners left at least one pet behind when evacuating their homes (ASPCA, 2021). Nearly 40% of these owners couldn't return to their homes for a minimum of four days. The pets left behind were exposed to harsh conditions, including minimal access to food or water, and exposure to predatory wild animals.

Here are the five components that ensure survival of your feline family member during a cat-tastrophe:

1. Visibility

We expect our pets to make a run for it if there's a natural disaster, but the sad reality is that most pets hide when they're scared. Moreover, first responders are often oblivious to the presence of pets in the house. You can prevent this oversight by pasting rescue alert stickers in a visible area outside your house. This informs the rescue workers of the number and types of pets in the home, so they can save the helpless animals.

2. Conditioning

Training cats to get inside the crate or carrier on command can speed up the evacuation process. A cat that responds to its name or comes running to its owner on command stands a better chance of making it to safety. You can also practice emergency drills with them so they're better prepared for unseen circumstances.

3. Emergency kit

Having a well-stocked emergency kit ready to go is crucial for a quick, seamless evacuation process. Your basic emergency kit may include flashlights, back batteries and first aid, but with pets on board you need to add a few extra items:

- Portable food and water bowls
- Cat carrier
- Cat food
- Portable litter box
- Emergency numbers for the vet
- Leash and harness
- Feline first aid kit
- Water bottle
- Cat litter or paper towels
- Your pet's medical records
- Microchip records
- Liquid dish soap

4 . Identification

A name tag and microchip are necessary for identification and may play a crucial role in reuniting you with your beloved pet. A microchip comes in handy especially for cats with the habit of wiggling out of their collars. It lasts a lifetime and can be scanned to access the biodata of your pet.

5. Convenience

Make sure the emergency kit is easily accessible and clearly visible during a quick evacuation by anyone who might need it. The most well-equipped emergency kit becomes useless if it's buried deep in the closet or some other area you can't reach easily.

The Takeaway

Your cat needs your care and affection the most during old age. Being patient and kind toward them as they grow old is the best way to show your love. Don't feel discouraged about taking in an elderly cat. You may have to tweak your methods slightly for an older cat with medical conditions, but training them is absolutely possible.

Traveling with your feline companion may seem challenging; however, with the right preparation you can turn the nightmare into a dream. Regular vet visits can help identify problems early and ensure your cat's health. If vet visits make your cat's anxiety shoot up, try handling it the way the doctor would in the comfort of your home. Eliminate its fear of the carrier by leaving it out as much as possible.

Your feisty cat may come off as clever and independent, but lacks the skills to develop disaster plans to protect itself in emergency situations. Remember that your pet depends on you for its survival needs such as food, shelter and medical care. It's our responsibility as pet parents to attend to our pets basic needs and ensure their survival.

With their adorable snuggles and endearing purrs, cats fill our lives with joy. All they ask for in return is that we take care of them when they need it most.

8

Building a Strong Bond with Your Cat

"I used to love dogs until I discovered cats."

– Nafisa Joseph

Getting Kiki to like me wasn't easy. Treats and toys could only get me so far. She'd growl and hiss whenever I did anything that displeased her, which was often. Cuddling her was out of the question. She'd swat at me whenever I tried. Her grumpy attitude was a problem, but I remained hopeful that I could get through to her.

Your relationship with your pet should be more than teaching them a few tricks. Building a strong bond with your pet animal involves nurturing trust through effective communication. In this chapter, we'll look at the importance of sharing a strong connection with your pet.

Your Russian Blue may not show the same fervent admiration as your neighbor's Golden Retriever, but that doesn't mean it's incapable of love, affection, and loyalty. As domestic pets, cats thrive when they feel close to their owner. Building a strong bond with your cat will lead to a multitude of physical and emotional benefits. Prioritize nourishing and maintaining a good relationship with your feline friend and you'd be surprised by how easy it is to train them.

Nurturing A Strong Pet-Owner Bond

Winning your cat's affection can be tricky. They are, after all, rather complicated creatures. Some may appear independent and apathetic; however, it is possible to win their approval and establish a positive relationship. Flaunting haughty personalities fit for royalty, their unique requirements and behaviors set them apart from other more docile pets. With a good understanding of the feline psyche, you have a better chance of getting your cat to toe the line.

Nurturing a healthy relationship with your whiskered friend is an ongoing process. Let's look at each monumental moment in your cat's life and how you can use the opportunity to strengthen your bond with them.

Purr-fect Beginnings

The first few days following your cat's arrival are crucial. It's natural for them to be a little frightened and shy as they settle into their new home. It may be helpful to limit their access to one or two rooms in the beginning with the food and water bowls within their reach. Provide them plenty of hiding spots where they can curl up and feel secure. Gradually, allow them to explore the remaining house.

Breaking the Ice

While exploring its new home, your cat will slowly warm up to you as its new owner. Gaining your new pet's trust may take some time. Be patient, allowing them to proceed at their own pace. Small gestures, such as stroking their fur when they approach you, can go a long way.

Avoid forcing them to interact with you. Grabbing them for a cuddle when they're not ready may just terrify them and undo any progress you've made. If you have children in the house, teach them not to rough house the new cat or kitten. Gradually, introduce your pet to the family members and make sure your cat always has the opportunity to run and hide if it wants to.

Cats respond positively to a consistent routine. They view disruptions with suspicion and may perceive them as a threat. It's important to introduce them to a new routine or changes in their surroundings in small doses. Let them take their time to accept changes.

Nurturing Through Nutrition

A well-fed cat, whose nutritional requirements are taken care of, is more likely to stay in a good mood. Finding your cat's preference may take some time, but once you've figured out what they like, make it a regular item on your menu at least for the first few weeks. Make subtle changes to their diet, widening their taste palette while attending to their nutritional needs.

If you need them to put on weight, increase the portion size slowly, offering plenty of variety. A robust diet packed with vitamins and nutrients will contribute to your cat's health. Though it's important to give your pet a varied diet, try not to change their meals too often. Frequent diet changes could be the culprit behind an upset tummy. Introducing new foods slowly prevents stomach problems while minimizing picky eating.

Don't be alarmed if your cat prefers a certain food item or texture over others. Some cats may enjoy wet food while others prefer dry snacks. Others still may prefer a combination of both!

Feline Fitness and Health

Physical, emotional, and mental health are a prerequisite for establishing a strong relationship with your cat. Regular vet checkups are essential for detecting problems early. Keeping your cat up to date with its routine vaccinations can help prevent a range of medical issues.

Daily walks outdoors could provide your cat the exercise it needs while puzzle feeders and indoor play time provides the mental stimulation it requires. A cat suffering from anxiety or stress is less likely to prioritize connecting with its owner.

Easy access to basic necessities such as regular meals and a comfortable place to sleep help boost your cat's confidence. Similarly, teaching your cat valuable skills such as using the litter box or operating the food dispenser instills independence, contributing to their mental and emotional well-being.

Decoding Cat Affection

It bears reminding that cats are not the same as dogs. Like the saying goes, "Dogs have owners, cats have staff." While they may come off as aloof, cat parents know how loving they can be ... when they're in the mood. The trick lies in understanding cat language.

It's important to note that while some gestures are common to every cat, each one communicates in its own unique way. Also, when we talk about cat language, it doesn't mean purring, meowing or growling. A significant method of communication in cats involves body movements such as blinking, tail twitches, or flicking the ears. We discussed basic cat nature in Chapter 1. Let's take a closer look at the different ways cats show their affection, so you understand your little munchkin better.

Slow Blinking

Is your cat perched next to you on the couch? Is it looking up at you and blinking slowly? If so, then you should be feeling flattered. It's the closest thing you can get to "I love you" from your cat. This is your cat's way of telling you that it trusts you. It feels safe and relaxed when you're around. Even though it's best to avoid staring at your cat, which they could perceive as threatening, try blinking back and see whether it blinks in response.

Head Butts

No, your fuzzy fighter isn't trying to take you on. Cats like being stroked around their head or their chin and may often bump their head against you to tell you they need petting. It could also be their way of saying hello or an attempt to leave their scent on you. They could be trying to tell you that they see you as its own. Gently tickle them under the chin or scratch behind the ears.

Showing Their Backside

When your cat presents its backside and perks up its tail, it could be asking for a spa treatment. Blow gently and voila! They think you're a cleaning master, and off they go!

Kneading

You're sitting comfortably on your couch. Your cat comes to sit next to you and, before you know it, you're getting a free massage! You should feel flattered if your cat starts kneading you with its paws because it's the highest compliment you'll ever get from your feline friend. They're treating you like family, trying to get some milk. While this may seem weird, it's their way of saying, "You're paws-itively awesome!"

Licking

Don't be alarmed. Your cat isn't trying to tell you that it finds you delicious. Licking their owner is an expression of love. They're grooming you to mark you as part of the squad. You've got to look your best to join the ranks of them. Don't forget to thank your cat for the glow up!

Sniffing

Does your breath smell? Why is your cat in your face all of a sudden, sniffing away? Your beauty obsessed kitty isn't checking for bad breath, it's doing something much sneakier. This is its way of leaving its scent on you. This is the perfect time to check your cat's teeth, especially if your cat doesn't let you examine its mouth. You can use moments like these to get your cat used to you checking its gums and teeth, making brushing their teeth easier.

Cat Chat

Respond to your cat's meows and purrs. Cats are talkative creatures and love a back and forth conversation with their owners. Meow back or make up what they're trying to say, you'll be surprised by how frequently you get it right! Ask them a question and guess what they're thinking in response. Greet them when you come home with a friendly "Hi" and scratch behind the ears. Join them in their singing sessions! Make use of these small opportunities to connect with your cat and make it feel included in your life.

Tail Position

The tail is your cat's mood indicator. When they're happy, their tails are held up high. When they're anxious or frightened, they hold it between their legs. If you catch them whipping or thrashing their tail around, watch out because they could be furious!

Get to Know Your Cat

Cats have different personalities. What is your cat like as an individual? Is it moody, like my Kiki, or calm, like my Zoe? Does it like being petted on the head or are tummy scratches their thing? If they detest being stroked on their belly, then rolling on their back and showing you their stomach may not be an invitation for you to stroke it so tread at your own expense. You might get nipped or swiped in response!

Spending quality time with your fuzzy feline will help you learn its likes and dislikes. Even if your cat appears strong and independent, it can feel lonely at times. While it may not make them cling to you constantly, it could make them yearn for your presence in the house.

Knowing that you're around might make them feel calm and relaxed. Similarly, the predictability of a consistent daily routine will make them feel more safe and secure. Here are some ways you can connect with your cat, get to know them better, and boost their emotional well-being:

Play

Cats love playtime whether their kittens or senior cats. However, each cat has its own preference. Kiki loves playing with cardboard boxes. She'd hide in an upturned box, watching anyone passing by, and launch into attack at our feet! On the other hand, Zoe has a quiet nature and prefers playing in the corner with her favorite stuffed mouse.

Chasing and catching is a cat favorite since it requires the use of their natural hunting skills. Playtime is an excellent opportunity to bond with your kitty. Regular play sessions can be as short as ten minutes and still prove invaluable. Avoid using laser pointed toys. Your cat might find them rather frustrating when it realizes it simply can't "catch" the light.

Figuring out what your cat likes or dislikes is part of the fun. Once you know what sorts of games your cat enjoys, you can make a routine of it. Make sure you've got all the supplies (cardboard boxes, squeaky toys, or ping-pong balls) and set aside a few minutes each day to play with your cat.

Grooming

Cats take meticulous care of their fur and enjoy being groomed by others as well. This makes grooming a great way to bond with your cat and get them used to being held by you. Regularly brushing your cat's coat gets rid of dead fur and skin, preventing hairballs and matting.

Training

Teaching your cat new skills can also be a great bonding experience. Short, fun sessions with lots of treats will keep your cat entertained and build trust. Be gentle and patient with your cat and you're sure to win their respect and approval. Don't expect your feisty feline to fall in love with you instantly. Gaining your furry friend's affection takes time and quite a bit of effort, but it's something you won't regret. Once you've laid down a strong foundation of trust, you're off to a good start.

Get Down to Their Level

No, I won't tell you to bow down to your meowster—though, I'm sure your cat won't mind. Cats prefer being on the same level as the person they're interacting with. This is why you may notice them climbing up the tabletop or the kitchen counter to catch your attention. Kneel down so you're on the same level as your cat during training sessions or when offering cuddles. You can also pick them up and place them on a raised platform such as a cat tree so they're at eye level.

Cat Pheromones

If you seem to be dealing with a particularly difficult feline, consider using cat pheromones. As we learned in Chapter 7, pheromones are natural chemicals released by cat's when they feel happy or relaxed. Your cat may rub its head or body against furniture or different areas in the house to leave its scent or pheromones behind. While humans are unable to detect these chemicals, cats are extremely sensitive to their presence. Artificial pheromone diffusers can lower anxiety in your cat and make them feel more relaxed in your company.

Avoid Punishment

Punishing cats for undesired behavior usually makes the problem worse. Cats are not designed to understand punishment by connecting it to their actions. At best, frequent mistreatment may give rise to anxiety issues or feelings of mistrust toward their owner. Although a loud "No" is sometimes necessary to grab your cat's attention and prevent them from causing harm to themselves such as chewing the electrical wire, try not to make shouting at your pet the norm.

Avoid scaring your cat on purpose. What may seem like fun and games to you or someone else, could end up terrifying your feline friend. Cats detest unpredictability as it makes them feel unsafe. Startling or scaring your cat for laughs destroys their trust in you. Dealing with an anxious pet is not worth a few seconds of supposed fun and some may even perceive such antics as plain cruel.

If you see someone else mistreating your cat in this manner, step in and stop them. A few years ago, my young nephew made a game out of stepping on Kiki's tail while his family stayed at my house for Christmas. The boy was too young to realize the trauma he was causing the poor cat. I had to sit down and explain to him the correct way to interact with cats and how much fun it could be. The boy ended up learning an important lesson about showing kindness toward animals and Kiki soon warmed up to him.

Give Your Cat Free Reign

As much as it matters for you to safeguard your house, it's important to give your pet ample freedom to explore its surroundings. This doesn't mean giving your cat free reign to unleash destruction on the living room couch with its murder mittens. Whenever you bring a new piece of furniture or change the home decor, let your cat familiarize itself with it while keeping a close eye to avoid any damage. If you spot your cat taking a swipe or attempting to scratch, say "No," pick it up and place it near the scratching post. Giving your feline some time to act on its natural instincts outdoors could also reduce feelings of frustration and boost their overall health.

Cats are natural explorers. Creating safe spaces in your house where your cat can reign supreme could also increase feelings of belonging and improve their relationship with you. This doesn't have to be anything grand. A small corner in the room where they have their bed, food and water bowl would suffice. Here, they could lay down for undisturbed naps or bring back small treasures from their trips outdoors.

Less Drama, More Love

Helping your cat face stressful situations means you'll be dealing with less drama. Doctor's visits, travel, getting into the carrier, or bath times could be a trigger for some cats. By taking these problems head on, you can avoid unnecessary flare ups and maintain a healthy relationship with your kitty.

Most cats are terrified of going inside the carrier or visiting the vet. In Chapter 7, we discussed how you can help your cat overcome these fears. Leaving out the carrier and getting your cat used to being handled are some ways to help alleviate your cat's stress. Avoiding situations that test your patience through a proactive approach will inevitably have a positive impact on your relationship with your cat.

Give Your Cat the Attention It Needs

Cats are high-maintenance. In their defense, they don't pretend otherwise. They love being fussed over and doted on. They crave attention, making them desire your company more than anything else. Spend quality time with your pet or include it in your activities when it's safe.

When you dedicate time and attention to your cat, it's like adding sunshine to their world. Cats thrive on affection, interaction, and the feeling of being valued members of your household. Your attentive presence is crucial for their emotional well-being. Spending quality time with your cat fosters a deep bond. It reassures them, creating a sense of security and trust. This not only impacts their emotional health positively but also influences their behavior. Cats that get plenty of one-on-one time with their owners tend to be more confident, affectionate, and less prone to stress or anxiety.

Your time and attention serve as mental stimulation for your feline friend. Engaging in play, gentle strokes, or even a quiet moment of companionship stimulates their mind, preventing boredom and potential behavioral issues. It's like a mental workout that keeps their cognitive skills sharp.

Cats may have built a reputation for themselves of being headstrong and independent, but they are social creatures that value their owner's presence. Your company provides them with love and attention they need, reducing feelings of loneliness or isolation. The time you devote to your cat shapes their emotional landscape profoundly. It enhances their happiness, reduces stress, and creates a harmonious bond between you and your beloved pet.

The Takeaway

If you're struggling to build a strong bond with your new cat, remember it's a slow process that takes time. Let the relationship take its course as you take small steps each day to win your cat's trust. You can set yourself up for success by prioritizing your cat's health. A cat that's well looked after has fewer reasons to complain. Adequate nutrition will not only keep your cat in a happy mood, it also prevents a number of illnesses.

Understanding your cat's language and decoding its behaviors is the key to having a happy cat. Follow a predictable routine, so your tiny furball doesn't feel thrown off by surprises. Keep drama to a bare minimum by helping your cat cope with stressful situations. Avoid harsh punishments at all costs and treat your kitty with love and kindness to establish trust.

Your relationship with your cat should be more than a few playtime sessions when you're bored. Learn their quirks, speak their language, and make them feel cherished. Value those special moments with your cat and never hold back on the cuddles!

9

Cat Training Success Stories

The past ten years I spent working with cat owners introduced me to a number of unique problems. At times, I found myself close to giving up, but with a little brainstorming, I could always find a solution to crack the most difficult cases. I realized cats are sensitive creatures that simply require a little patience in the beginning. Once trust is established, they could prove to be your most loyal companion.

So far, I've told you a lot about Kiki, now let's look at some success stories of my clients. Get ready for whisker-raising adventures about feline training triumphs. In this chapter, we're diving deep into the heartwarming tales of cat guardians who cracked the code on training their whiskered wonders.

These stories are about the magic that happens when dedication meets determination. Get inspired by the feline feats achieved by cat enthusiasts worldwide. Whether it's mastering the art of litter box finesse or getting your kitty to high-five on command, these stories showcase the incredible bonds formed through patience, creativity, and a sprinkle of catnip-infused motivation.

So, grab a comfy spot, a hot cup of coffee, and prepare to be enchanted by remarkable examples of cat-human teamwork that'll leave you feline fantastic!

From Feral to Friend

The Calico Cat and It's Three Babies

When my client Martha discovered the Calico and her three kittens in her jeep, it was love at first sight. Believed to be a sign of good luck in many cultures, Sunny, the Calico, was a hissing and spitting machine. Soon, Martha started finding it impossible to get her to leave her jeep let alone show any kindness toward its owner. Taming Sunny left Martha feeling exhausted. Everyone advised her to give up. Sunny was a lost cause, but there was hope for the kittens.

"Taming her is impossible!"

"It'll take years!"

"Just get rid of the cat and keep the kittens."

Luckily, Martha understood the reason behind Sunny's aggression and felt sympathetic. After all, she was trying to get Sunny to leave the place she considered home. It was no surprise the new mum took Martha's well-intentioned interference as a threat. The jeep was familiar to her and she was ready to put up a fight against the stranger who tried to take her somewhere unknown. Moreover, it was possible her previous encounter with humans hadn't been pleasant.

The thought of giving up on Sunny and the kittens was inconceivable for Martha. She knew that abandoning the family could have disastrous consequences. Rescue groups in her area were working at full capacity and didn't have room for one let alone four cats. The fact that Sunny had given birth in her jeep made her feel responsible for her welfare.

With leaving out of the question, she decided to try everything to make things work. This is when she contacted me about the ordeal. Together, we devised a plan to get Sunny and the kittens out of the jeep. At first, she wouldn't let us come near or touch any of the kittens. It took a few days to gain her trust. Even then, she looked anxious when we picked up the first kitten and transferred it to the basket. Soon, we managed to bring the entire family indoors.

However, this wasn't the end of our struggle. Training Sunny was difficult. We went through numerous ups and downs. She'd make progress one day only to regress the next. One step forward, two steps back—that's how things went on for quite some time.

Martha was riddled with doubts. She kept wondering how much longer it would take to get Sunny to like her. Was it even possible for them to be friends? With a little motivation, she'd pick herself up and get back to training Sunny and her pack.

During the mornings and evenings, we tried to get the cats used to having Martha around. She'd spend as much time as them at these times as possible and reward the cats for taking kindly to her presence. Slowly, Sunny started lowering her defenses. Martha and I learned to celebrate the small wins, taking things one step at a time. But once we discovered Sunny's weakness: salmon flavored treats. Finally, we'd found our magic key! Suddenly Sunny started showing more interest in the training process.

Each day, we felt like we climbed another rung on the ladder, coming one step closer to our goal. Gradually, Sunny started trusting us more. The day she finally ate from Martha's hand came as a relief. She caught us by surprise a few days later when she jumped onto Martha's lap. The day she rubbed her face against Martha's almost made us both cry. The cat that used to hiss at anyone who came near the jeep couldn't resist cuddles anymore! The feral Calico that refused to be tamed in the beginning now wanted to snuggle with her owner all the time.

It's been four months and Martha is amazed by how far she's come with Sunny. She is loving and gentle. She meows politely for food, thoroughly enjoys Martha's company, and hops onto her lap for morning cuddles before breakfast. She doesn't like being held for too long though and Martha is working on that. What matters the most is that Sunny has accepted her new home. She and the kittens are part of the family.

Most people shy away from adopting stray cats but they can prove to be remarkable pets. All these cats want is a home of their own and a loving family. I truly believe there's no such thing as an untrainable cat. We should never underestimate what can be achieved with a little patience and lots of love. While the road may be wrong and bumpy, the reward makes the struggle pale in comparison.

Turning Foes into Fur Buddies

The Siamese and Labrador

This is a heartwarming tale of cat and dog teamwork! Simba, a confident Siamese cat, found his world flipped upside down when Buddy, a chill black Labrador, came trotting into the house one day. The two animals' pet-parent life turned into a bit of a juggle, with Simba fearing Buddy, making it tough for the two of them to share space and time with their humans.

A little pheromone magic and some positive reinforcement did the trick. Buddy learned relaxation moves so he could tolerate his feline pal, while Simba got a confidence boost with some clicker training. Slowly, they met through a baby gate, Simba got his high perches, and voila! The bonding began.

And guess what? Simba and Buddy are now a dynamic duo! They're inseparable, especially at chow time, where cheese and fish bring them together in a hilarious team-up. From foes to friends, their bond kept growing with more training and TLC. Simba's okay with Buddy's face licks, and Buddy's cool with Simba's purrs.

Their parents even think they're secretly kindred spirits! So, can cats and dogs really get along? You bet! With the right training, fun intros, and a dash of good management, these two show us that harmony is totally paw-sible!

From Scared Stray to Family Hero

Persian Cat Saves Owner

When Kevin started fostering Finn, getting hissed and spat at wasn't exactly what he expected. But that was his introduction to Finn – a large, scared community cat. Rescued alongside 23 feline friends, Finn found his way into Kevin's care. He'd never experienced much human contact before, only being fed by one of the neighbor's a few times. He was frightened of everything new. But today, he's a whole different cat! He's the boss of the house, overseeing four felines, three playful dogs, and three caring humans. He makes sure everything is just right.

Finn loves to lie with Kevin in the study and jumps onto the bed for a cuddle. He nuzzles his head against Kevin's chin, purrs contentedly, and sometimes enjoys a belly rub. He's especially fond of Kevin's Kelpie Cross, Buster!

While training Finn was an uphill battle, he proved to be more than just a loving pet. He actually saved Kevin's life from a potential house fire! When Kevin was down with the flu, Finn persistently jumped on and off him until he woke up. Kevin followed him into the kitchen where he smelled smoke – he had accidentally left the stove on, and it was moments away from causing a fire.

Thanks to Finn's alertness, Kevin was able to avert a disaster. From that moment on, Kevin knew Finn was meant to be with him. He's seen Finn transform from a scared cat to a relaxed house companion. Timid cats, like Finn, just need a bit more time to trust. It's been an incredible journey to watch them grow and become a part of the family. Kevin is considering giving other timid cats a chance – they might just change someone's life!

Community Cat Whisperer

Turning Feral Cats Into Lap Loungers

My neighbor Katy had a love for cats. She noticed numerous stray cats in her area and decided to feed them. At the onset, most of the cats Katy fed scattered as soon as she entered the patio with their food. They only approached once she left. So Katy decided to change her approach. She sat on the floor, trying to appear smaller, positioned far away from the food bowls, and patiently waited.

Week after week, Katy stayed, motionless, as the felines slowly approached, cautious and wary. She avoided any movement until they left. This routine persisted for many weeks. Gradually, she edged closer. Over time, she managed to move around without startling them. After months of consistent effort, some cats allowed her to play with them using toys and treats.

To build trust, Katy used baby food on a long wooden spoon, gradually bringing it closer to the cats until they were comfortable eating from her fingers. They also enjoyed playing with wand toys, relishing these interactive moments.

After around six months of dedication, a breakthrough occurred. When Katy arrived with food, she was greeted with leg rubs, raised tails, and joyful prancing. Some even perched on her lap, showcasing a newfound trust and companionship.

Oliver's Journey

Scared Ginger Learns to Trust His Pet Parents

Oliver, a hefty, ginger tom, found himself in a state of crisis, urgently needing to leave his former home, a warehouse. Joy and Matt were approached to foster him, drawing on their experience with timid cats. But none had been as frightened as Oliver. Initially, Oliver was an epitome of fear and resistance. He stared with unblinking eyes, hissing, spitting, and swiping at them with claws bared. His fear was palpable; a slight push could lead to a painful bite. Every chore around Oliver was a tense affair. Cleaning his litter tray or placing food and water meant dodging his claws and lunges.

Necessity inspired innovation. To protect themselves while easing his terror, they devised meticulous safety measures. Instead of a soft igloo, a large carrier was his sanctuary within the crate, furnished with a heated bed and secured carrier door.

When they needed to reach in, a garden stake acted as a buffer, preventing potential lash-outs.

Food was offered through a stick, ensuring safety while affirming that they were the bearers of sustenance. They introduced a "taming wand" to gently stroke Oliver through the wire, gradually acquainting him with touch.

After painstaking efforts, Oliver started to relax. His demeanor shifted from guarded hostility to occasional moments of contentment, closing his eyes in trust while being touched by the wand. The breakthrough came after months of patience – Oliver permitted gentle strokes with their hand, a remarkable milestone that left Joy and Matt overwhelmed with joy.

While he still shied away from direct touch in the crate, Oliver found solace in the presence of other cats. When allowed into a room, his demeanor changed remarkably. He played, relaxed, and trilled with happiness, a far cry from his fearful self. The turning point was when Oliver dared to leap onto their bed. It was a touching gesture, a symbol of trust and acceptance. They savored this moment, cherishing the honor of his choosing to be near them.

Yet, Oliver's fears lingered. While he enjoyed playful interactions, their hands remained a source of unease. When the couple consulted me, I speculated about Oliver's ingrained fear, possibly rooted in his genes, passed down from his ancestors. They accepted Oliver's limitations, allowing him the freedom to explore the house, although his fear persisted. They considered returning him to his original outside home, but the idea posed risks. I suggested letting Oliver be, allowing him to carve his sanctuary within their home.

Today, Oliver thrives in their care, comfortable in their presence as long as touch is with a wand. His sanctuary is a safe haven, sharing space with feline friends, cherished, and cared for. While adoption might not be his destiny, Joy and Matt find comfort in knowing that Oliver is loved, safe, and allowed to be his true self.

Grace's Marathon

A Journey with Lucy and Jasper

Grace, a dedicated marathon runner, encountered a life-changing moment during one of her routine training runs. A small white flash darted past her on a dark, stormy morning, scuttling into the dirty, disused underground toilets at a supermarket. Despite her efforts, the cat remained out of reach, hidden amid the filth in the stairwell.

For three months, Grace attempted in vain to seek authorities' assistance to rescue and rehome the cat. Each disappointment fueled her determination to ensure the cat would have a better life. Through her relentless determination, she managed to convince the Council to allow her to catch the cat herself. Connecting with a rescue group, finally led to the successful rescue of the infamous kitty during the early morning hours one Sunday.

The cat was in dire straits. Now named Lucy, her white fur was stained, matted, and filled with dirt by living in the trash for so long. She was infested with fleas and smelled awful. Her condition was simply heartbreaking. Grace dedicated herself to transforming Lucy's life, naming her after the supermarket employee who assisted in her capture.

Lucy began her transformation journey in a spacious dog crate, while Grace meticulously recorded every significant milestone. Small victories, from grooming to responding to treats, brought Grace immense joy. The moment when Lucy finally allowed Grace to pet her was emotional.

By week five, Lucy showed remarkable progress, greeting Grace at the front of the crate and seeking affection without the need for food bribes. Her exploration of the spare bedroom marked a significant step, leaving behind the crate that once served as her sanctuary. Lucy's playful and energetic nature delighted Grace, who couldn't resist bending her house rules. The "no animals on the furniture" policy was long forgotten as Lucy claimed her space on the spare bed.

Week eight brought more triumphs as Lucy let Grace pick her up, signaling her readiness to meet Olive, Grace's dog. Eventually, Lucy and Olive became housemates, spending weekends together at Grace's beach house. Their companionship blossomed over time. As their bond grew stronger, Grace decided to adopt a three-month-old kitten, Jasper. Following the same method used with Lucy, she socialized Jasper from scratch before introducing her to the sanctuary room.

Five months later, Lucy and Jasper had become inseparable best friends, sharing moments of play, sleep, and grooming. Grace even modified her house to provide them with safe outdoor space, witnessing their joy. As Grace continues her runs, she often passes by the place that was once Lucy's home, marveling at how much her life has changed. Lucy, now a gentle and beautiful cat, has found her forever home with Grace.

The Remarkable Rita

Feral Kitten To Loving Companion

A tiny, stray kitten started appearing on my porch in the mornings a few years ago. She looked no older than 8 weeks. I fell in love with the tiny kitten but she remained elusive, only stopping to take a quick bite from my cat's food bowl before dashing into the garden.

Other than being hungry, she seemed otherwise healthy. It would quickly gulp down food and vanish without attracting attention from the other neighborhood cats, who may have chased her away if they'd happened to notice her. Even to this day, Rita remains lightning-fast.

A few weeks later, I saw Rita roaming around with another cat from the colony. Surprisingly, this cat had taken the kitten under his wing. This companionship involved protection, guidance, and exhilarating games, along with accompanying the older cat on his territorial rounds and skirmishes. The newfound friendship made Rita gain some confidence. She started appearing more frequently, with the older cat tagging along for a free meal.

Disaster struck, when one day the duo was attacked by other cats. I managed to rescue Rita, but she didn't seem too happy about being deprived of the freedom to patrol the streets. I settled her into a puppy crate in the bathroom. In the beginning, she shied away and remained wild, dashing into hiding at the slightest approach. Continuous efforts involving frequent visits gradually started showing results. At last, she stopped hiding during meal times.

When she finally started feeling comfortable with me in the room, I encouraged her to begin interacting with the other cats. They engaged with her through the crate bars in the beginning.

Eventually, Rita started playing outside the cage with the bathroom door closed as a precaution. Slowly, she was allowed more freedom, interacting with other cats and, over time, allowed me to pet him. As I brought her to the bedroom, Rita slowly adapted, feeling safe enough to play and interact, often bringing a ball for me to throw. Gradually, she became more at ease, welcoming cuddles and play sessions.

Exploring the larger house, Rita relished the freedom during the day and spent time outside in a protected garden mesh. Over time, her confidence grew, becoming a joyous and friendly addition to the household.

The now transformed Rita ended up finding a new home just two days after being posted for adoption, where she was interviewed by potential adopters and has since settled in beautifully. Her remarkable journey from a shy, wild kitten to a friendly and playful cat showcased the transformative power of patience, companionship, and understanding.

The Takeaway

These stories show the transformative power of patience, compassion, and understanding when it comes to taming and nurturing feral or timid cats. The journey of these remarkable felines, from their initial fear and wildness to their eventual trust and companionship, highlights the dedication and perseverance of their caretakers. Katy, Kevin, Joy, Matt, Grace, and others taught me the importance of unwavering commitment, creating safe spaces, using innovative methods, and gradually earning the trust of these cats.

From rocky beginnings, these cats finally experienced warmth, kindness, and love of humans. Through persistent efforts these gentle creatures were able to bridge the gap between fear and trust. Each cat's unique personality and journey resonated with the caretakers, leading to notable changes, be it Finn's life-saving act, Oliver's slow but steady progress, or Rita's remarkable transformation.

Through patience, consistent efforts, and a deep understanding of feline behavior, these caretakers allowed their cats to bloom, encouraging their socialization and eventual integration into their homes. They adapted methods, from using toys and treats to creating safe spaces, proving that every cat's journey to trust is unique and rewarding.

The stories of Finn, Oliver, Rita, and Kiki are not just tales of cat-human interaction but reflections of hope, resilience, and the power of compassion. They remind us that every cat, no matter its initial fear or wildness, has the potential to flourish if it's provided with the right care, patience, and love. The bonds formed between humans and these once-frightened cats shed light on the changes that can occur when understanding and empathy triumph over fear and doubt.

Conclusion

We started our journey by understanding cat behaviors. We learned how these adorable furry creatures can turn into formidable warriors when their territory is challenged. Then discovered their obsession with keeping themselves looking pristine through grooming and their hunting instincts modeling their unique personalities. Taking cues from your cat as you set out to train them guarantees success.

Sometimes, our furry pet's adorable faces don't match up to their ferocious nature. Simply labeling these loving creatures as problematic and giving up on them is easy. However, it means we won't get to experience the immense joy of helping these animals heal. Creating a positive environment, predicting their behavior, and using positive reinforcement are some methods to bring a stop to the drama and lay the foundation of a strong pet-owner relationship.

Preparation is a must before you dive into training your cat. Change your perspective and drop down to your cat's eye level. You may see obstacles and temptations you would've missed standing up. Begin cat proofing your house one room at a time. Once you've taken all possible hurdles out of the way, you can move on to preparing your training toolkit. Food pouches, a huge bag of treats, clicker devices, target wands, scratching posts, litter boxes, harness and leash are some must-have items for your inventory. If you're short on budget, you can get a little crafty and build your own scratching post, litter box and target wand.

While you're out shopping for your cat, don't forget the grooming supplies! A few combs and brushes can keep your cat looking picture perfect.

Now that you have everything you'll need, it's time to get down to business and let the training commence! Realistic targets will prevent you from getting discouraged and keep the training process fun and interesting. Start with basic obedience training, teaching your cat simple commands such as sit, come, gentle play, target, and in the box.

Keeping the sessions short, offering multiple rewards and irresistible treats will increase your chances of success. The process will not always be as rosy as you'd like and you'll most likely run into a few bumps along the way. Giving the training a break, offering new rewards, or addressing any other problems your cat may be facing can help you overcome plateauing progress.

While you're busy teaching your new cat to respond to your commands, don't forget about litter box training. Kittens take to using the litter box easily compared to somewhat older cats. However, that doesn't mean cats can't be litter trained in later stages of their lives. Getting the right litter box and litter is what counts the most. Senior cats with arthritic problems may not respond well to containers with raised walls. Lids and hoods may trigger claustrophobia in some cats. Clumping, non-clumping, and odorless litter can impact your cat's response to litter box training.

If you're worried about keeping your furniture secure from those murder mittens, then trying out strategies to alter your cat's behavior could be the answer. Avoid punishments and harsh treatments at all costs as they can have a serious impact on your cat's mental and emotional health. Start by offering your cat alternatives, using a bit of catnip to get them to move on to the scratching post, or introducing scratching posts with the same texture as the object of their fixation.

Other strange habits that may spring up with cats include spraying, chewing fabric, and excessive grooming. For all these problems, effective solutions usually involve a combination of positive reinforcement techniques and offering alternatives. Stressed and anxious cats cause more problems than others, so getting them treated is the best option.

Once you've got their problematic behaviors in check, you can move on to advanced training, which includes teaching cats to jump through hoops, roll over, respond to your call, fetch, and high five. You can make your relationship with your cat less strained by helping them cope with stressful situations such as vet visits, problems associated with old age, anxiety, and emergency situations.

Underlying health issues could be the culprit behind a number of problems related to the litter box, increased aggression, excessive grooming and vocalization. Ignoring your cat's health can lead to disastrous consequences, so always make regular checkups by the vet a priority. Your cat has only you to depend on, so make sure you're there for them when they need you the most.

As the pages of this book draw to a close, it's clear that training cats is not just about teaching tricks or obedience, but a combination of understanding, patience, and mutual respect between human and feline. Within these chapters, we've explored the complexities of feline behavior, delving into their innate instincts, unique personalities, and art of communication. From decoding their body language to understanding their preferences, we learned about the depth of their intelligence and the nuances of their interactions.

The tales shared within these pages—of cats overcoming fear, of building trust, and forming unbreakable bonds—underscore the incredible potential for growth and connection between humans and their beloved feline companions. The journey from timidity to confidence, from uncertainty to trust, echoes the power of patience, consistency, and compassion.

In each story, whether it's about coaxing a once-feral cat into a loving home or understanding the subtleties of communication to facilitate learning, a common thread emerges: the beauty of the human-cat relationship lies in its ability to transcend barriers, fostering deep connections built on empathy and understanding.

This book isn't just a guide to training cats; it's a celebration of the intricate and wonderful world of feline companionship. It's a reminder that training isn't just about the end goal of a command learned; it's the journey that matters, the moments of breakthrough, the mutual trust forged, and the growth, both for the cat and the human.

My hope for you, as you close this book, is that you carry forward the lessons learned—that training a cat isn't about bending their will but understanding their nature, that patience is a virtue, and that the most profound rewards come from the simplest gestures of love and understanding shared with our feline friends. For in the world of cat training, it's not just the cat that learns, but the human that grows in compassion and connection.

References

ASPCA. (2021, September 13). *New ASPCA Survey Reveals 83 Percent of Pet Owners Live in an Area Impacted by Disasters, Yet Less Than Half Have a Preparedness Plan in Place.* Retrieved December 21, 2023, from https://www.aspca.org/about-us/press-releases/new-aspca-survey-reveals-83-percent-pet-owners-live-area-impacted-disasters

Greene, N. (2018, November 6). *My cat's clothes-eating obsession has to stop.* Cat Life. Retrieved January 4, 2024, from https://slate.com/human-interest/2018/11/cat-eats-clothes-stop-advice.html

Hodgson, S. (2022, May 19). *Cat Training: 7 Commands to Teach Your Cat.* Daily Paws. Retrieved November 19, 2023, from https://www.dailypaws.com/cats-kittens/cat-training/cat-training

Printed in the USA
CPSIA information can be obtained
at www.ICGtesting.com
LVHW012115250124
769471LV00084B/3385